MW00893533

# STEP UP

*The Key to Succeeding in
Male-Dominated Businesses*

## ROSEMARY YEREMIAN, M.A.

authorHOUSE

*AuthorHouse™*
*1663 Liberty Drive*
*Bloomington, IN 47403*
*www.authorhouse.com*
*Phone: 833-262-8899*

*Book cover designed by David Moratto*

*Published by AuthorHouse 03/25/2021*

*ISBN: 978-1-6655-1786-7 (hc)*
*ISBN: 978-1-6655-1787-4 (e)*

*Library of Congress Control Number: 2021903682*

*Print information available on the last page.*

*This book is printed on acid-free paper.*

# CONTENTS

# AUTHOR'S NOTE

This book is a labor of love. For the past twenty-five years, my female colleagues and I vented our frustrations about having careers in male-dominated fields.

We faced similar obstacles, regardless of region, country, stage of career or company. We worked with a variety of industry associations and corporate groups to improve the situation. However, many of us felt that we still had a long way to go.

In February 2020, I traveled to Ottawa, Canada for an energy conference. During that trip, some friends named John and Brigitte invited me over for dinner. Both had worked in high positions in the energy sector. We were hanging out in the kitchen while John made dinner. Brigitte and I compared notes about some of the ridiculous situations we had faced as women in male-dominated workplaces. As the laughter and tears subsided, I confided that I was thinking of writing a guide to help women succeed in male-dominated business sectors. Brigitte, in her bubbly way, immediately jumped on the idea. "Oh my God! That's a brilliant idea. I know at least ten women who would want to help!" And that's how it started.

As I began writing and telling people about the idea for the book, more and more businesswomen came forward and offered insights and anecdotes. I was overwhelmed and humbled by their responses. Almost every woman I spoke with wanted to contribute. Their stories were heartfelt, empowering, sad and moving all at the same time. I wish I could have included every story in the book. They wanted to help other women believe in themselves and "*step up*" to the challenge of succeeding in business.

In this book, there are no fictitious names nor events. The events I describe really happened. Where a person's name appears, their permission has been granted. In all instances, accuracy was my goal. I reconnected with the people involved in the described events and asked specific questions to ensure my being devoid of personal bias.

Some opinions in this book are probably not universally agreed upon. The views I expressed do not necessarily represent the views of the people who contributed their stories. The book's views are my own.

Wherever possible, I have tried to use language that is friendly and less "business-like." I was going for an approachable, warm, conversational tone.

*Step Up* is meant to empower women to succeed in male-dominated businesses. The reason this is needed is because there continues to exist a certain cohort of men who are more "traditional" in their behavior at work. Some women may find these "traditional" perspectives offensive and outdated. The vast majority of the men I encountered in business do *not* fall into this category. They are confident, supportive and collaborative. The book addresses being able to thrive in an environment where both types of individuals exist.

My expertise in the subject comes from twenty-five years of experience in the Aerospace, Energy, Defense and Nuclear Energy sectors. I have a Master's Degree in Political Science from a non-ivy league school. I live modestly on a salary that is well below what I think I'm worth. I am a single mom raising two kids. I have worked hard, struggled and persevered to get where I am today, and it has not been easy.

I hope the lessons learned and the guidance in this book provide a solid foundation for women around the world to fully believe in themselves, and to know they are worthy of success.

*Rosemary Yeremian, December 31, 2020*

# CHAPTER 1
## Stepping Up and What It Means

Let's face it. Being a woman in a male-dominated field is hard. Like, really freaking hard.

Anytime 75% of the workplace is made up of men, things are just *different*. Everything is a competition. Women struggle to get their voices heard. We are often talked over, ignored, dismissed, or told we "don't have what it takes."

It's no wonder that so many highly educated and skilled women shy away from these industries. Even when we do enter these fields, succeeding seems next to impossible. Climbing Mount Everest is nothing compared to a woman trying to succeed in a male-dominated business.

Yet, some women--a precious few, actually--are taken seriously and make it to positions of power. They somehow become vice presidents, presidents and CEOs, despite facing every workplace disadvantage imaginable.

It's not that these women didn't face what the rest of us have faced. It's not that they are superhuman or blind to what goes on. What they did was something different. They broke through the glass ceiling. They stood at the top of the hill and said to the world, *"I will not be ignored."* They had something valuable to give. When they stepped up to bat, they swung and swung and swung until they finally hit a home run.

What was their secret? How did they beat the odds and succeed? Most importantly, what were those crazy ninja moves they used to get around the obstacles that are constantly thrown in the way of success?

I've spent my 25 year career in male-dominated fields, and let me tell you: It wasn't easy. It's not easy. I was subject to bullying. I was ignored at meetings. My ideas were dismissed without reason. I was passed up for promotion countless times, while my less skilled male colleagues moved ahead. And, yes, the sexual harassment was unbearable. I wanted to give up so many times, and I almost did.

What I've learned is that there is a way to break through. There are strategic and tactical ways you can work within the system and get ahead. Trust me. I did it.

If you saw me, you'd understand why this was a freaking miracle. I'm less than 5 feet tall and (relatively) slim. Having olive skin and black curly hair didn't help. My Master's Degree in Political Science could have been a piece of toilet paper in the eyes of my engineering and trade finance banker colleagues.

Yet, I found a way to step up and get noticed. I stepped up by volunteering for projects. I stepped up by working harder, longer and smarter than everyone else. I stepped up by refusing to sit in the back row against the wall when there was no room around the boardroom table. Instead, I pulled one of those back chairs up to the boardroom table and made room for myself. I stepped up by making sure that everyone I met in the business world knew me and was impressed by me. But the biggest lesson I learned is to step up by finding key strategies and tactics that helped me work within the system to get ahead.

And now I want to share those with you. I want to throw down the gauntlet so that you too can succeed. I want to show you a number of strategies and tactics that you can use to get ahead in whatever male-dominated sector you work. Because I know you can.

If you bought this book, you are already invested in your success. Why? Because you are taking action. You're not settling for less. You are making an effort to stay in your field and find ways to march through the craziness to succeed and lead. And I want to help you get there.

But first, an example from my own experience . . .

**Stepping Up in Action**

When I was 25, I got a job with a government-owned export finance company. Part of my responsibilities included advising the financial-service managers on the international rules of trade finance and then I went to Paris, France, to negotiate those rules.

It was my dream job.

After spending the first few months advising our internal bankers about the international rules, it was finally time to fly to Paris and help update those rules. I would be representing the federal government. I can't tell you how nervous I was on that airplane. My palms were sweaty. I couldn't sleep. Once we arrived at our hotel in Paris, I started poring over my research and notes in preparation for the negotiations the next day. The negotiations were aimed at coming up with a new Agreement to include private market indicators into an existing international regulation.

It was my first time at the international negotiating table. Before the trip, I had prepared my information and spent countless hours researching how we could achieve market rates for government-backed export loans. I now had to convince the countries around the negotiating table to follow my suggested approach. This was not going to be an easy task.

At breakfast, my hands were shaking as I held my croissant and downed my café au lait. My colleagues told me to let them do the speaking—to sit back and listen. During the morning negotiations, my male colleague successfully made the case for what I was championing by reading my carefully drafted speech. As he read the speech, I watched for reactions around the room. It was a large room in the old-Parisian style of grand salons. The tables were in-laid with green leather and gold, and arranged in a giant square. Every country's representative had a place at the table. As I watched, I could tell that the other people around the table seemed wary of my idea, but they were willing to consider it.

I had prepared by building a relationship in advance with the people who worked in the international organization. They were open to my ideas of what to include in the new Agreement and asked a lot of questions. We covered in advance the various strategies I could use for the negotiations, and someone suggested I have ready responses to the trickier questions that would inevitably come up. This helped me in two ways: my colleagues at the international organization got to know me and my ideas, which brought credibility to my ideas and recognition to me personally, and I learned in advance what I would be faced with so that I could prepare my responses.

At lunchtime, it was suggested that a few delegates meet and hammer out the agreement while the others ate. Because the people at the international organization knew I had all the technical knowledge for my idea, I was asked to stay behind and work on a new draft of the Agreement with the small group.

I stepped up to the challenge. I immediately said *yes*. My boss Klaus looked at me like I had three heads. He eyed me carefully and said, "Are you sure you're up to this?"

I said, "Yes! You go have lunch and when you come back, we'll have an agreement." He and my colleagues reluctantly left.

As soon as the door closed, I turned to face the sharks. I knew I was in way too deep to back out. We were led to a smaller room with a computer and four chairs. It was me, the US delegate, the British delegate and Mike, the young, cocky American who worked at the international organization. As nervous as I was, I stepped up to sit beside the computer as we started to draft the new Agreement. I was ready. I had already prepared the agreement in my mind and had written drafts in my notes and in my head.

As we spent the next hour thrashing out the new agreement on Private Market Indicators, I started to feel more and more secure. At the last minute, the British delegate turned to me and said, "Should we add something in there about what Klaus was talking about?" I enthusiastically agreed and we included a clause in the agreement that I knew would make him happy.

Klaus returned early from lunch to read the final agreement. As he sat at the negotiating table, I couldn't read his expression as he carefully paged through the document. Suddenly, he looked up at me. "Rosemary, this is really good. I'm very impressed!"

I responded, "I even added a little present for you in section four. You see? That part about quarterly reviews." His eyes widened.

It took all of one hour (lightning-speed time in international negotiations) for the country members of the international organization to agree and sign on to the final draft.

*Bam!* I had just rocked the world of international trade finance.

Did I mention I was 25?

**How did I Step Up?**

First, I had an idea that I knew was fantastic. I knew that by looking at what the private banks were doing, we could provide export loan prices that were reasonable for the risk involved. But having the idea alone wasn't going to get me anywhere. I then had to do a lot of research to show my idea would work. Based on facts, evidence and trends, I showed my colleagues and bosses the benefits of my recommendation.

Once they agreed internally to the solution, I had to prepare to sell the idea to a roomful of wary international representatives. I stepped up by introducing myself to the people who worked at the Secretariat of the international organization where I would be negotiating. This included: the policy advisor and the head of the division. I telephoned them, asked them about their jobs, about the people around the table. I asked about their families. I wanted them to see me as an ally. Once I established a relationship, I could get pointers from them about how people would react to my idea.

I then prepared for the meeting. I had all necessary facts and figures. I came up with potential objections to the idea and answers to these questions. I wrote the speech that my boss would give and armed him with the information he needed in advance, including objections and responses. Five days before we flew to Paris, I stepped up again by suggesting a meeting where we combed through the notes and speeches in order to make my boss feel comfortable with what he was going to say.

Finally, when the opportunity arose to close the deal, I took it. I was prepared and capable, and I had made sure that everyone around me knew it.

At every stage of the process, I stepped up by being prepared, building relationships and proving my credibility through my knowledge of the facts and figures. I managed to find a way to work within the existing environment to gain influence and succeed.

## Why Do We Need to Step Up?

As women in male-dominated industries, we need to step up for two reasons. First, I believe businesses thrive and grow when the entire staff is highly engaged. Having a team where people cooperate and collaborate is better than a competitive environment where everyone is striving to win a gold medal.

The second reason is more complicated. Women are often given the short end of the stick when it comes to excelling in male-dominated industries. Because traditional stereotypes about women are still widespread in these sectors, we face high levels of discrimination and lower levels of career support and mentoring. All this can lead to high stress levels, great anxiety and low self esteem. As a result, many women in these fields tend to get discouraged and either quit or settle for staying in a low-level position.

When this happens, there is a negative effect on the woman's mental health, family, loved ones and ultimately the company.

I want to encourage women to step up for both these reasons. We deserve to have our voices heard and to stand out based on our merit. When we are treated as equals, everyone wins. But we are the ones who have to get ourselves there.

## What Does Stepping Up Mean?

Stepping up is about carving a path forward for yourself where none exists. It is about taking control of the narrative of your career, and playing an active role in your future success. When I asked my female colleagues on LinkedIn what they thought *stepping up* meant, they said:

> "I think I step up and volunteer for new projects and initiatives." – *Nuclear energy professional*

> "Think outside of the box and challenge some of your most basic assumptions. If your business model is X, ask yourself if you can expand to Y and what the barriers are. Definitely try new projects, but also explore areas that you would not traditionally explore. Get inspiration from some of the agile organizations that are used to pivoting as times change; a recent example is some of the restaurant chains that are now providing meal kits. What a great idea and quick way to make up some of the market loss through Covid.¹" – *Engineering lab executive*

In business there are many ways to step up. For me, stepping up means taking action in such a way as to successfully influence the desired outcome. It means:

- Being clear on what you want to achieve
- Feeling deep down that you deserve to be a successful leader
- Developing influence by understanding the male decision-making processes
- Having a deep understanding of the necessary technical data
- Working with mentors to determine how to get ahead

7

- Volunteering to take on key initiatives and activities
- Demonstrating confidence
- Taking credit for your accomplishments

The chapters of this book will take you through these eight aspects of stepping up.

## Why I Wrote this Book

They say that if you can't find a book on a specific subject, you should write it. This is what led me to you today. I got frustrated at the lack of support out there for women in my situation. I decided to do something about it. I summarized what I had learned and reached out to get the thoughts and opinions of other female leaders in male-dominated industries around the world. I was overwhelmed by their responses. Almost all wanted to contribute their experience and lessons learned. They wanted to help put together something that could show women how to succeed in these industries.

This rag-tag bunch of female executives, directors and managers had a lot to say about the subject. They enthusiastically shared their stories. Some of them were sad. Some were funny. Most of them, though, were phenomenal. They all overcame the crazy stuff we have to deal with on a day-to-day basis, and they succeeded.

I wanted to tap into their secrets. I wanted to write a book to show women that we are not alone in facing the unique challenges that come in businesses that are predominantly male. Not only are we not alone; there are specific ways we can "step up" and get ahead of the game. This book is all about showing you how to succeed in male-dominated industries. I use practical examples, stories and strategies to get you on the path to achievement.

Over the coming chapters, I will share the key strategies and tactics for getting ahead and excelling as a savvy businesswoman in male-dominated industries. And don't take my word for it. Throughout the book, I've included input from female leaders in these fields. Their stories are relatable. I hope they will inspire you to find your own path to success.

# CHAPTER 2

## *Navigating the Male Psyche*

If you are anything like me, you probably want to find a way to succeed in a male-dominated business based on merit and without compromising your integrity. There is nothing like success based on knowing you deserve it.

The challenge with male-dominated businesses is that things are not as straightforward as we would like them to be. We need to first understand the workings of the male mind to navigate there.

Men see things from a certain perspective. The more we understand that perspective, the better we can handle ourselves within that context. I don't mean to excuse behavior that we may find offensive. But, if we understand where a man is probably coming from, our reactions can be more meaningful in response to certain behaviors.

The first thing we must recognize is that certain patterns of behavior occur in male-dominated businesses. These patterns shape the culture of these businesses and how they operate.

This chapter will discuss some of these patterns and give you tactical ways to navigate through them.

### Competition Is the Norm in Male-Dominated Businesses

How often have you raised a topic with your male colleagues only to have them go on *ad nauseum* about their views on the topic as they understood it, *whether or not you had finished talking?* Although "mansplaining" in business can make women doubt their knowledge or feel like we need to prove ourselves, it is important to understand that this happens for a reason.

Do you ever notice how much men take credit for their work in male-dominated businesses? Men are amazing role models in this regard. They take credit for the smallest win. They manage to make everything look so easy. They speak with such confidence and purpose. It can be overwhelming. Sometimes, it seems like so many men are vying for attention and credit that our voices get lost. However, if we are too loud, we are called "aggressive" and "bitchy." It is such a double-edged sword trying to navigate people's perceptions of us as knowledgeable and assertive, while at the same time being considered "good" team players.

Getting your idea across in male dominated fields is quite different from how it is in more gender-equal industries. When men make up much of a work environment, competition becomes the norm. Why? I wish I knew. I have noticed that there is something about a roomful of men that makes them want to one-up each other and prove themselves, while putting others down. Maybe it is a territorial thing. Whatever it is, we must recognize and accept that everything will be a competition in male-dominated fields.

I have found that when men are mostly in the presence of other men in business, they tend to feel the need to prove their masculinity. Competition goes into high gear and the idea of compromise is minimized.

Have you noticed that if you bring up a new idea, it is often shot down by those who did not think of it first? If it is not shot down, it is ignored and then brought up later by a male colleague who takes all the credit. Some days it seems next to impossible to get your ideas across. However, with some crazy ninja navigating, it *is* possible to get your ideas across, even amid the competitive atmosphere.

To adopt an idea from someone else in this context, men often need to feel they came up with *part* of the solution. The more they influence the direction of a decision and add their own imprint, the more likely they are to support it. The same goes for work activities. If they play a role in a particular task, they are more likely to participate. Perhaps they need to have some stake in things so that they can claim victory.

At first, I thought men were competitive *only with women,* which is why some men treat women as less than deserving. I mean, didn't I see it happening all the time? Weren't my female colleagues complaining about this incessantly?

It turns out, I was wrong. As I was talking to a male colleague about it, he said, "But Rosemary, don't men do that all the time? Even to other men?" My mind was blown! Of course! Men compete mostly with each other in business to get ahead. It is not something reserved for women. Maybe they are being aggressive because they need to compete with everyone to get ahead.

I started to wonder . . . if this was the case, then maybe I should not take being put down personally. Maybe it was not me. Could it perhaps be that this is the way men are programmed? Maybe I needed to learn how men process new information and how they make decisions. Based on that, I thought, surely, I could figure out a way to navigate the noise and get the credit I deserve.

Based on these insights, I figured, there must be a way to handle myself tactfully and elegantly so that I get the most recognition and value out of my work. And that is what I did. Using these insights made me much less offended in the workplace and much more active in whatever I was doing. I learned to co-opt my male colleagues into a joint effort that they could brag about, rather than sit back and complain that things were not fair.

I want to share some ways I found to "Step Up". You can use what I learned to take a different approach to your work life. I hope that by sharing these ideas, you too can develop leadership skills and succeed.

## Avoiding Stereotypical Roles

In highly male-dominated sectors, traditional stereotypes of women can reign supreme. Whether it is fetching coffee, making photocopies, or cutting the cake at a work social, women tend to be pigeonholed into these roles regardless of their position or title. Most times, our colleagues do not even realize they are doing it. It may be a subconscious force of habit for them. Maybe it is even another way to assert their position in a competitive environment. Whatever the reason, there are ways we women can bypass these stereotypes and get around being treated as a stereotypical female.

Stereotypes in the Boardroom

Have you ever been asked to take notes at meetings, while your male colleagues seem to never get asked? This drives me crazy. For some reason, people assume that because you are a woman, it is your responsibility to take notes for everyone.

---

In Her Words . . .

A very brilliant Vice President of an electric utility that I worked for asked his departments to establish objectives and strategies for their functions. I was assigned to help these highly paid managers develop these crucial management tools. I was sure many of them intuitively did these for their specific functions, but I had already learned that unless staff were engaged participants and committed players, the objectives of the company would not be won.

I joined a meeting in progress with these nine senior, experienced, well educated managers. The first question I was asked was this: "Do you take meeting notes?"

I only had one response and it emerged from my mouth immediately. "No, they didn't teach it in Graduate School."

*Marion Fraser, former Chief of Staff for a Government Department. Sector: Energy*

---

I love the way Marion handled the note-taking question in the above story. Not only did she let people know it was not her place, but she also emphasized her high degree of education. There are other ways to handle the question of note taking as well:

- Suggest that an administrative assistant sit in the meeting and take the notes.
- Have a different person take notes for every item on the agenda.
- Use rotation so that a different person takes notes at every meeting, ensuring that the responsibility does not lie with one person.

Although the above suggestions are for taking notes, they can also be used for fetching coffee, making photocopies, cutting the cake at work parties or any other menial chore that is below your status. Whatever it is, making sure the responsibility for these chores is shared is one way to deflect the task from you alone. You did not get to where you are today by making coffee. You deserve to be treated better than that. Let them know that and hold your head high.

The *only* time I will offer to take notes in a meeting is when I want to influence the outcome. They say whoever holds the pen holds the power. I have found this to be true. So, when I do take notes, I ensure that action items are noted, and the meeting notes reflect the discussion around the table. However, the meeting notes will often emphasize certain things and de-emphasize other things that are in my personal best interest. It is a dog eat dog world in male-dominated businesses. So, if we absolutely must take notes, let's do it in a way that maximizes our desired outcomes.

Stereotypes at Conferences and Trade Shows

Consider, for instance, the experience of a friend of mine, who is a Project and Proposal Manager for companies that do business with the US Department of Energy National Laboratories.

In Her Words . . .

I was at a conference for the first time with this company I worked for. As we drove to the hotel from the airport, we were going over the plan for the day, including itineraries for the week, sessions we wanted to attend during the conference, and after-hours meetings we were attending.

I learned on this car ride that I would not be attending any of the sessions. I found out that in fact I had been brought to the conference to be the booth "babe" and answer questions about the company I had started working for 5 months prior. I was not invited to any of the after-hours meetings with my male colleagues, and I would be setting up and taking down the booth on my own while they attended pre-scheduled meetings.

I sat in the back seat of the car in silence, with small "mm-hmms" occasionally. I was shocked, but what could I say? Then I was given instructions on how to set the booth up, including step-by-step instructions on how to put the poles together, which included internal bungee cords that snapped the poles together. I was so embarrassed to think they thought I was not intelligent enough to 1- read the instructions included in the packages and 2- put poles together that literally did not come apart.

I was dropped off at the hotel to gather some additional booth materials and then walked the 3 blocks to the convention center while they drove off in the rental car. I proceeded to put the booth up as I had been asked and went back to the hotel to work on a proposal that was due the next day.

When the time came to go back to the convention center for the opening ceremony, I was left at the hotel to walk the three blocks to the convention center. I was embarrassed, intimidated, and unsure, but I put on my convention face, introduced myself to as many people as I could between the opening ceremony and heading in toward the booth. I did not do much speaking to my colleagues the remainder of the conference and vowed that I would never be left out again.

*Randi Johnson, Project and Proposal Manager. Sector: Nuclear Decommissioning*

I cannot begin to tell you how many times I have seen companies hire "booth babes" to drive in traffic at trade shows and conferences. In the past, many companies hired young women to stand in their booths and attract visitors. I have seen these so-called "booth babes" wearing tight white bikinis and flaunting their flesh. It is disgusting, and it makes things harder for the businesswomen in booths to be taken seriously. A businesswoman should never be put in that position.

So, how can we avoid being treated this way at conferences? We need to "Step Up" our level of engagement. Here are a few tips that I would recommend to ensure that your male colleagues recognize your place as a valuable attendee at conferences and trade shows:

*Before the conference:*

- Offer to take care of logistics. Then, create a schedule for booth duty for each person attending the show. Ensure that there are always two people in the booth, if possible, preferably one male and one female. That gives you enough time to attend the sessions and meet potential customers, which is what you are ultimately there for.
- Set up meetings with potential customers in advance. That way, if your male colleagues assume you will be in the booth the entire time, you can let them know that you have business and meetings to attend to that are for the greater good of the company.

*At the conference:*

- Ask your colleagues for help in setting up the booth. This does two things. First, it lets them know that setting up the booth is not only your responsibility. It is better for them to think that you do not know how to read instructions and set up a booth than to assume it is your responsibility. It's as easy as saying, "Look, setting up this booth is not part of my job description or yours. Let's do it together so that we can both learn." Secondly, it puts you on equal footing with your colleagues. If you are setting it up together, it becomes a team effort and not just your burden to bear.

- Walk around the trade show floor and meet as many potential business leads as you can. Invite them to your booth to learn more. When they come to your booth and ask your boss for you by name, it will show your colleagues that you are a serious businesswoman who is recognized by people in the industry.

*After the conference:*

- Send an email to everyone you met saying that it was a pleasure to meet them. You can also send your company brochure, offer to help them with something or follow up on some questions or leads. Most people don't do anything with the business cards they collect from a conference. Yet, people remember those that keep up communication with them afterwards.

**Being Recognized as an Equal**

I recall an experience at one international meeting. A new woman joined the Power & Operations committee. In a boardroom of 20 people, there were only 4 of us that were women. So, we were ecstatic to have another woman in the group. She was highly qualified and had lots of experience to share with the committee. She was also very dynamic, and I was sure that she would be an active member who could help move things along.

During the committee meeting, the past chairman kept referring to her as "the new girl." He was a respected older fellow in his mid-60s who had been involved in the organization for a long time. After he had called her "new girl" about three times, some of us started to correct him and say, "Her name is Catherine." To our shock and amazement, the past chairman continued calling her the "new girl." Toward the end of the meeting, we learned that she had been a nuclear operator and that her technical and management experience was far greater than the past chairman's. I am not sure if he ever learned her name. Afterwards, a group of us went to the conference organizers and complained about his behavior.

Being overlooked is commonplace for women in male-dominated businesses. There are times when we are made to feel like we do not exist. How do we handle things when people are ignoring us?

The answer lies in the concept of "Stepping Up." The sad truth is that when people overlook us, we tend to allow that to happen. We keep quiet and let nature take its course. Perhaps we are too shy and fearful of what would happen if we spoke up. Maybe we think our bosses and colleagues would think less of us. But "Stepping Up" is exactly what we need to do.

The next time you are about to walk into a meeting, consider how you intend to show up. Are you going to show up meek and quiet? Or are you going to go around the room and introduce yourself to everyone while handing out your business card? I know it can be intimidating. Just remember that you deserve to be seen. You deserve to have your views heard.

Here are some other ways you can be recognized:

- Keep a logbook of your accomplishments. Show them to your boss on a regular basis, especially during performance reviews.
- Put aside any fear and introduce yourself to people in your company, even if you do not work with them. The more people you know, the more you will learn and get ahead.
- Offer to host a *Lunch n Learn* on a topic that is near and dear to your heart, or a lesson you have learned from your work.
- If you are meeting with customers, make sure they know your name and have your contact information. Follow up with them after the meeting and offer to answer their questions.
- Ask your boss what you can do to increase your profile in the company. You may be surprised by their answers.
- When in doubt, use humor. A little humor can go a long way toward getting recognized by a group of male colleagues who are overlooking your participation. Keep it professional and funny.

In Her Words . . .

In 1997, I was selected for a United Nations Peacekeeping Mission to Guatemala (MINUGUA) and I became Canada's first female United Nations Military Observer (UNMO). For this particular mission, I was also the only female in the 155-member contingent made up of Spanish speaking officers from around the world. Generally speaking, the Latino culture tends to have very strong forms of gender norms in terms of the customs and beliefs that the members of the community share towards masculine and feminine. And this mission was no exception. Besides the pressure of demonstrating that I could do my job effectively, I had the added challenge of navigating their expectations of what they deemed suitable for me in my role as an UNMO. Overall, respect, confidence and a good sense of humor were critical to managing these situations. I was simply not prepared to have my participation in the mission marginalized or minimized because I was a female.

*Eva Martinez, Executive. Sector: Aerospace and Defense*

## Dealing with Mansplaining

If only I had a dollar for every time I raised a topic, and one of my male colleagues went on and on about something that had nothing to do with the topic. "Mansplaining" happens when a man explains something in a way that is condescending or patronizing to a woman. It happens a lot in business. It happens even more in male-dominated sectors. Usually, it comes from a need to clearly demonstrate that they have more experience and knowledge than you. When a man "mansplains," he often interrupts or talks over his female colleague to explain something she already knows. I have seen women with PhDs in engineering be mansplained by someone with far less education.

What is the reason for "mansplaining"? We must look again at the competitive environment that is the foundation of male-dominated businesses. When a man interrupts a woman, who is speaking about her own expertise, they are implying that she is ignorant. The assumption is that she is not capable of having authoritative expertise about the topic at hand. Essentially, it is a sign of disrespect and men's way of proving they know better.

Being on the receiving end of "mansplaining" makes us feel like we do not know enough or that we do not have enough know-how. For many situations, unless a woman has explicitly asked a man to explain things for her, it is not welcome and can be demeaning. It can even affect how we handle ourselves professionally by making us meeker and quieter.

What do we typically do when we are "mansplained" to? If you are like me, you tend to let them finish. After all, it is rude to interrupt someone, right? Typically, we sit patiently and smile until it is time to move on. But what if you do not want to be treated this way?

I believe it is high time we stop putting up with this behavior. We need to Step Up and be clear that this sort of conduct is not welcome.

Here are some ways I have learned to deal with "mansplaining":

<u>Be firm</u> - If you haven't finished talking and someone interrupts you and goes on and on about something unrelated to what you were going to say, I often raise my right hand with my palm facing towards them. It is a small gesture that is meant to say "stop." I then explain that I have not yet finished talking and that I would like to hear their opinion but only after they have listened to what I was going to say without interruption. It can be as easy as saying, "Hold on right there. I was not finished talking. I do want your views, but only after I have finished saying what I need to say. If you can just hear me out, I can get to the part where I need your opinion."

<u>Redirect</u> – Suppose you start a conversation, and your colleague interrupts you to take it in a totally different direction. Is it okay to interrupt them and redirect them to the original conversation? You bet it is. Stopping the tangent and bringing everyone back to your original point is important if you want to be successful. Sometimes I say things like, "Stop for a minute. That is not what we are talking about. I would like to draw your attention back to the matter at hand. We were talking about X. I'd like to continue

that conversation before we start talking about things that are not related to it." In a not-so-subtle way, you are telling your colleague that they were going off-course and that the matter at hand is what needs to be talked about. By re-directing, you are not only taking control of the conversation, you are also demonstrating your authority.

<u>Show Your Worth</u> – When mansplaining is done in a condescending way, you need to address it upfront. Do not let them get away with putting down your level of knowledge or expertise. Prove your worth. Do not be shy about demonstrating what you know. When this happens to me, I usually say something like, "Perhaps you didn't know I've worked in the nuclear power industry for 20 years," or "Your comment makes me realize that you are not familiar with my background on this topic. Let me explain to you the expertise I have in this area." Briefly outline your expertise and continue your discussion.

<u>Talk Louder and Do Not Let Them Interrupt</u> – This can be a bit tricky at times because the female voice can be softer than a man's. I have seen it work though and have used this technique with much success to my surprise. The next time a colleague interrupts you, try not letting them. Keep talking in a louder and clearer voice. Even if they continue, do not stop. The person who interrupted finds himself interrupted and in a losing position in the competitive world of male-dominated fields.

<u>Use Humor</u> – Everyone loves humor. Humor is a powerful weapon. Use it to your advantage. Sometimes, a well-placed quip with a smile is all you need to shut down someone trying to mansplain to you. It is a softer and subtler way of handling the situation that, when done right, can put the culprit back in his place. Just make sure you smile while you are doing it so that it comes off as jovial rather than irritating. "Johnny, I know you always love letting everyone know your opinion, but I'll keep going so you just have to wait until I'm done." Adding a wink in there helps.

Navigating the male mindset is all about recognizing the competitive nature of stereotypical men and feeling empowered enough to face it head on. Allowing yourself to fade into the background while your male colleagues compete with each other to get ahead will never give you the influence you need to be successful. By Stepping Up and using a variety of tactics to reinforce your value, you will start to earn the respect of your colleagues and start to succeed in ways you never thought possible.

In the next chapter, we will talk more about increasing empowerment by reprogramming your belief systems.

# CHAPTER 3

## Re-Programming Your Belief Systems (Damn it, You Deserve Success!)

When I started to succeed in business, I found myself doing strange things. Maybe you can relate. We would have a meeting and I would recommend a course of action. Then, just before the meeting ended, I would ask the staff, "Is that okay?" I would wait for their response. Usually, they would say *yes* and I would end the meeting.

It must have sounded weird to them. Why was I doubting my own recommendations? Why was I asking for their approval? Could you imagine a male colleague doing this? Absolutely freaking not! I imagine that any male colleague I know would likely direct his staff to take a particular course of action and then ask them to report back to him when they had completed their tasks. I began to wonder why I wasn't acting in the same way.

Even when we know what we are doing, and we have lots of experience, we still seem to doubt our abilities. When it comes to believing in ourselves in business, we tend to be our own worst enemies either consciously or subconsciously.

Women across different businesses face this challenge. Several books, such as *Lean In* by Sheryl Sandberg, discuss how our own internal obstacles hold us back. Sandberg says that women keep themselves from advancing because they don't have the self-confidence and drive that men do. "We lower our own expectations of what we can achieve," she writes.[2] The lack of self-confidence and belief in our worth are key factors that hold us back from becoming successful leaders in our fields.

This feeling that we are unworthy of success tends to be worse in maledominated fields.

According to a *Financial Times* article written by Barbara Stocking,[3] women tend to be alienated and pushed aside in male-dominated workplaces. She outlines the challenges women face, including:

- Their voices are not heard
- They are interrupted or ignored in meetings
- Much work takes place on the golf course, at football games and other male-dominated events where women are rarely invited
- Progress is not based on merit and women have to do better than men to succeed
- In discussions about selecting people to move up the corporate ladder, questions are about whether a woman "is tough enough."

Being faced with any one of these challenges can wear a person down and result in a feeling that we don't deserve success or advancement. Highly qualified women may be led to believe something is wrong with them in this context. This belief can zap their confidence. In reality, absolutely nothing is wrong with them! You know as well as I do, that there is zero truth or evidence that women are unworthy or undeserving of success. They are being put in positions where they have to do some special crazy ninja moves to get ahead.

Have you ever been in this situation?

A friend likes to relate a story about a boardroom meeting she attended with eight men to discuss a key business challenge. My friend, let's call her Sarah, was (and still is) a hard worker who had spent a lot of time trying to solve this business challenge. As the meeting started, the men around the table dominated the conversation without even asking her opinion, despite the fact that it was her job to address this particular issue. Halfway through the meeting, she spoke up and outlined a recommended solution. As she likes to tell the story, "Everyone stopped for a moment and looked around, as if a little bird had chirped and they were all trying to figure out where the noise was coming from." The men then continued their discussion as if she had said nothing at all. After about 15 minutes, another man spoke up and raised the exact same point that she had raised earlier. All the other men congratulated him for his innovative idea and the meeting was adjourned with that course of action adopted. Her lack of confidence kept her from speaking up and correcting the situation.

Sound familiar?

The key question for us women in male-dominated field is: How do we prevent this lack of self-confidence? Or, how do we regain our self-confidence after it has been attacked? How do we learn to handle the everyday snide remarks about us and move ahead in our careers with grace and recognition?

**My Experience with that Nasty Ex-Boyfriend Called "Doubt"**

When I started out, I was young, short (still am, ha-ha), and female. I did not have an engineering degree or an MBA. My Master's Degree in Political Science was all I had. I was surrounded by tall men with technical degrees up the wazoo. In meetings, my male colleagues talked over me. When I raised my voice to be heard, I was usually interrupted or ignored. I felt helpless, small and unworthy of success. Tears were a regular part of my day. I knew I had something to offer and I was too afraid of the consequences to step up. Would I be overstepping my bounds? Was I expected to sit there and take notes? Shouldn't I be meeker in order to make my boss look good?

I sat down with an engineering colleague to complain. He listened carefully and then said, "Rosemary, it's not because you are a woman and short that people aren't paying attention to you. It's because you're not acting like you deserve it—even though you know your stuff inside and out." My mind was blown. It was true. I didn't act like I deserved success. I wasn't showing off my knowledge and talent because I was too scared. I felt it wasn't my place and that I had nothing to offer, which absolutely was not true. That was a real wake up call for me. I *did* deserve success!

So how did I get myself out of this crazy thinking?

Well, I did two things:

1. I changed the core negative beliefs I held about myself by lining up facts as to why there were untrue; and
2. I took action

Changing your beliefs is a lot harder than it looks. When I started to change my negative core beliefs, I had to face some very dark thoughts that I didn't know were there. I started to explore what those beliefs were and why I had them. The "Why?" was the most crucial part. I found that I was holding on to beliefs that had absolutely zero basis in reality.

Actually, when I held up facts against those negative beliefs, this crazy thing started to happen. The evidence showed that the exact opposite of my negative beliefs was true. I actually knew a lot! I deserved success based on my accomplishments. It turned out I was short-selling myself to the point that I placed myself below my male colleagues who had significantly less experience and fewer accomplishments.

That was a real wake up call.

Once I changed my negative beliefs and adopted empowering beliefs, things started to change dramatically. I no longer felt like I had to prove myself. I was more relaxed and happier. I floated around the office with confidence and a smile. I began to repeat this mantra to myself: "I know better." When people came to me with information that I knew was wrong, I would repeat my mantra to myself, take a deep breath, and calmly explain why the information was wrong. The old me would have gotten upset and argued with the person, leaving both of us frustrated and upset.

After that, taking action was easy. Once I had my new, shiny empowering beliefs, it became a no-brainer to volunteer for special projects and to offer to write reports. Soon, I had momentum going for me. It became a self-fulfilling prophecy. The more confident I was, the more work I took on. The more work I took on, the more I got noticed. My self-confidence started to soar.

---

In Her Words…

While in my first management position, I received a call from a head-hunter about a job elsewhere. I did almost everything possible to say that I was not qualified, but the head-hunter pushed me to at least accept the interview. I did, and that started my Management career.

Fast forward ten years and an old boss called me to offer me a position in Operations that he felt I would be perfect for. Again, I tried to talk my way out of being qualified. I met with him and then declined, suggesting I was not ready. Five years later, the same company approached me for a lateral move. I accepted that one right away. When I arrived, I realized that I could lead in an operational role. If I had trusted others' instincts about my abilities, I could have been here sooner.

As females, we underestimate our abilities and seem to be wired to think there is someone better qualified, or suited for that next promotion. I see this in the workplace often, that when a lot of females are asked about a different role, they first come up with reasons they wouldn't fit.

If I were to give advice to my daughters, it would be to never underestimate themselves. Hard work and humility will go a very long way and that we need to trust what others see in us because sometimes what we see in the mirror is not the full picture.

*Janet Wardle, President & CEO, MHI Aerospace Canada, a division of Mitsubishi Heavy Industries*

---

## Moving from Negative Self Beliefs to Feeling Empowered and Conquering the World

There are many ways to transform your beliefs from negative to empowering. Consider the world of psychology and Cognitive Behavioral Therapy. It has done wonders for me. If you find it difficult to let go of some deeply held beliefs, think about getting professional help.

In the meantime--instead of your spending years and thousands of dollars in therapy--I'm going to take you through a fast-track method of changing your belief systems. This system has helped me and many others.

### Reprogramming Negative Beliefs

Prepare a document with two columns. Label the first column: Negative Beliefs. Label the second column: Facts and Evidence Against the Negative Belief.

| Negative Beliefs | Facts and Evidence Against the Negative Belief |
|---|---|
|  |  |
|  |  |
|  |  |
|  |  |
|  |  |

Spreadsheets are a great tool for this exercise, but it can also be done in any software tool you prefer. A ready-to-go template can be found on my website: www.stepupinbusiness.com

Under Negative Beliefs, write your insecurities and negative beliefs about your prospects in your male-dominated sector. Here are a few of my own examples:

- I can't get ahead because I'm a woman
- People don't respect me
- I don't have the skills to get ahead
- I don't have the technical knowledge to get ahead

Once you have done this (and I know it looks depressing), take a look at your list. I'm sure writing this will be hard to do, but I promise there's good news ahead.

In the second column, and for *each* negative belief, I want you to write down the facts and evidence that make that negative belief completely irrational. The key here is: Be as specific and fact-based as possible. You'll amaze yourself.

Some examples from other women include:

- I graduated top of my class from Princeton
- I successfully wrote a report on how to increase revenues, which laid the groundwork for the company's business plan for the next five years
- I brought in 3 new customers this quarter with total sales of $500,000
- I won an award for Best Service
- My colleagues are always coming to me for advice, showing they respect me and believe I am successful
- I wrote and implemented Procedure X, which has saved the company 5% in regular expenses

At the risk of sharing too much information, I've included part of my list below. I'm almost ashamed at this point that I ever thought this way. But until I confronted my fears, that mental glass ceiling of my own making blocked my success.

| Negative Beliefs | Facts and Evidence Against the Negative Belief |
|---|---|
| | 1. I have been successful in the past by selling engineering solutions and by helping major engineering companies make lots of money. |
| | 2. I increased revenues by 50% in one year. |
| | 3. I built relationships with customers allowing me to significantly increase our business. |
| I will never be successful in business because I am not a man or an engineer. | 4. The new major customers I brought to my company in the military and aerospace sectors have brought us an annual revenue base of over $1 million. |
| | 5. I created processes and procedures allowing my company to run more smoothly and efficiently. |
| | 6. I acquired a $100,000 grant for my company. |
| | 7. I was voted to join several boards of directors and was hand-selected for another board. |
| | 8. My nuclear and aerospace colleagues view me as successful. |
| | 9. I won the Outstanding Service Award for an industry association. |

Take my list as an example. I had these crazy beliefs that I wasn't good enough to succeed. It was reinforced because my male colleagues treated me this way by ignoring my ideas or interrupting me when I spoke. This negative belief guided my every move and action. I felt paralyzed.

Once I started to write the facts and evidence against the negative belief, a light bulb went off. I was awesome at what I did. I started to see myself the way others saw me: Smart, Confident, Successful, Accomplished. Notice how I wrote down several facts (nine in this case) that countered my negative belief. Once I began writing the facts, I was on an unstoppable rollercoaster. New ideas about facts and evidence became obvious and countered my negative belief. I was on a roll.

After looking at the facts and evidence, I was amazed that I even had the negative beliefs in the first place. It was a real boost to my confidence.

**Creating Empowering Beliefs**

Now that we've quashed your limiting beliefs, let's replace them with new, empowering beliefs about yourself that will better serve you in terms of getting ahead in your field.

I'm a fan of lists, so we're going to continue with this approach.

The next thing you are going to do with your list is to *erase* the negative belief. You are now going to *replace* it with your new, shiny, empowering belief. Make it sound awesome. Make it a true reflection of who you are.

Now, create a new column where you list the positive things about you that make you worthy of success. Don't hold back. Think of every reason why you deserve--nay, command--respect and success. There's no limit. Write anything that comes to mind for the next 10 minutes. This template is also available at www.stepupinbusiness.com in case you want to use a ready-made example.

Here is how my new empowering beliefs look:

| Empowering Beliefs | Facts and Evidence to Support the Empowering Beliefs | I Deserve Success Because . . . |
|---|---|---|
| I am a freaking superstar when it comes to business | 1. I have been successful in the past by selling engineering solutions and by helping major engineering companies make lots of money. | 1. I'm extremely smart. I think faster than my colleagues. |
| | 2. I increased revenues by 50% in one year. | 2. I find patterns and trends in business that give me insight about future strategies to pursue. |
| | 3. I built relationships with customers allowing me to significantly increase our business. | 3. I bring real value to companies that results in significant new revenues and reduced expenses. |
| | 4. The new major customers I brought to my company in the military and aerospace sectors have an annual revenue base of over $1 million. | 4. I am a natural leader. |
| | 5. I created processes and procedures allowing my company to run more smoothly and efficiently. | 5. I contribute lots of ideas to make things better. |
| | 6. I acquired a $100,000 grant for my company. | 6. I have X degrees and Y certificates in five fields. |
| | 7. I was voted to join several boards of directors and was hand-selected for another board. | 7. Lots of people around me--including my husband, my kids, my colleagues, and my friends--believe I am successful. |
| | 8. My nuclear and aerospace colleagues view me as successful. | 8. My kids deserve a strong female leader as a role model. |
| | 9. I won the Outstanding Service Award for an industry association. | 9. I feel happiest when I am contributing to the growth of those around me. |

Congratulations on your list! You now have a list of factual and evidence-based data points that clearly outline how and why you are a superstar and worthy of success despite being in a male-dominated field! That's awesome!

**Visualize your Success**

When my son was born in 2007, I left my cushy corporate job to start a business development consulting firm. I wanted to work from home and have a flexible schedule. There was one problem though. I had never had to "sell" before. For the first time I had to hustle and generate sales of my own to keep the company afloat. I had to learn pitch techniques and the like. Moreover, I had to get over my limiting belief that these older guys in the nuclear energy field would not want to listen to little ole me—a non-engineer in heels.

I adopted a powerful technique when I started learning sales. My business coach at the time saw that my limiting beliefs were guiding my lackluster performance. He asked me to do a visualization technique that I use to this day. It is simple and has powerful results.

To use this technique, I had to do a visualization exercise before each pitch meeting. I had to mentally prepare and see myself in a position of success. In the visualization exercise, my business coach asked me to see myself in the meeting as if it were taking place. I visualized myself being confident and smiling. My presentation was excellent and thoughtful. The older, white men around the table nodded and said to me, "This is exactly what we need!" I then saw them handing me a 6-month retainer contract for a high fee. As we signed the contract, they kept telling me how they thought I was brilliant and how I was really going to help them succeed.

I would do this exercise before every meeting and every pitch. Now, not all of my pitches resulted in major contracts as a result of this technique, but I signed a significant number of new contracts. In addition, the people I pitched began to refer me to other people that they thought could use my services.

Within one year, my business went from being a startup and making $60,000 per year to making $400,000 per year. Sales started to excel after that, and within 4 years, I had a multinational consulting company with locations in 4 countries and some of the top companies in my field as clients.

Try this for yourself. The exercise is easy and requires no list.

Close your eyes and visualize yourself in a room of male colleagues where you are pitching an idea. If your main job is not pitching an idea, come up with another scenario where you are trying to influence these men.

Imagine outlining reasons for them to follow your idea. See yourself providing details and evidence that help your case. You need to be detailed in your visualization of yourself:

- What you are wearing (a suit perhaps? What color?)
- Are you standing or sitting nice and tall?
- Is your voice projecting confidence and assertiveness?
- Is the expression on your face calm and collected?

Now, imagine outlining your case for whatever it is you are trying to accomplish. Perhaps you see yourself giving a presentation. Perhaps you are taking attendees through a report you wrote about a new business idea. Whatever it is, see yourself going through the motions of presenting your case.

Imagine your male colleagues nodding their heads in agreement to everything you say. Imagine one or two of them asking difficult questions. Then, see yourself handling these objections with poise and elegance, providing more facts and figures.

Finally, imagine them standing and applauding your work. They are telling you how great you are and how they are so impressed with your ideas. Make it bigger than life if you can. Maybe in your imagination, they hold a parade for you after you leave the room. Maybe they ask you to become the vice president, or even better, president of the company. Maybe they want you to make speeches at conferences as a result of your power and influence.

Whatever you visualized makes you feel amazing, right? You can carry that feeling with you from now on. Anytime you feel in need of a boost, especially before big meetings, you know what to do.

Just take yourself back there and see it all unfolding the way you want *before* it actually happens.

Will reality always match your dream? Of course not. What's critical here is that you will now walk into that meeting with confidence and poise that you did not have before. This exponentially increases your chances of success in the meetings.

**Taking Action: The Final Step**

Now that you have reprogrammed your negative beliefs, created empowering beliefs and visualized your success, let's make that a reality.

---

In Her Words…

If a job posting goes up, a man will apply if he has only 30% of the skills. If a woman has 99% of the skills, she still will not apply. She does not believe she belongs within her own belief system, that she deserves that job. So, what happens when she does apply and gets the job? She finds herself in that boardroom and she still doesn't believe she belongs or is worthy of the position. She tries to fit in, is quiet, and perhaps no one will know of her fear of being found out. And this is the most astonishing fact as to what happens next. We as women get in the boardroom and then WE don't believe that other women belong. And it's a vicious cycle.

---

So, when I started my company called "SheIs", the vision was built around being positive with statements that empowered women and girls. The negativity will always exist. However, we were going to highlight the positive stories of women in professional sports. Our campaigns are all around women belonging and #WomenWorthWatching . And my message to you is very simple:

*You are the person that can make the difference in advancing women, not just in sports, but in anything you chose. It just takes action.*

You cannot get on your social media and go, 'Me too, I believe in it. Yes, I sponsor it. Yes, I go and watch.' It doesn't work.

*You have to take action to make change in this world.* You have to know that you are worthy, you are deserving, and you belong. Taking action is the only way to make sure change happens.

"ONE DAY" or "Day ONE" You Choose!

*Brenda Andress is the President and founder of SheIS and the Inaugural Commissioner of the Canadian Women's Professional Hockey League*

The fact is, no one gets ahead by sitting at their desk and simply doing their work. In order to be successful, we as women need to step up and take action. Taking action allows you and your colleagues to see your efforts and be recognized.

Action can take a number of forms.

- Show Interest: If you want to work on a project, volunteer for it. If you want to lead a team, tell your boss or another colleague that can make it happen. No one will appreciate your contributions until *you* appreciate them. Demonstrate to others that you can be relied on to step up and take the lead. By doing this, you'll show that you are a valuable contributor to the organization.

- Speak Up: Studies cited by the *New York Times* show women are much less likely than men to speak up in meetings when they are outnumbered by men. This is largely because they are interrupted, talked over, shut down or penalized for speaking out.[4] When they do speak up, they apologize repeatedly and allow themselves to be interrupted. If you don't believe you have anything worth saying, how will others have confidence in you? If you don't understand something at a meeting, ask a question. Recognize the value of your opinion and believe that what you have to share is worth hearing. Even if you get interrupted, keep talking. The minute you stop talking, you have ceded control.

- Show Confidence: As women, we often try to please others and we remain quiet. Sometimes, when we do talk, we do so in a soft, gentle voice that indicates we are unsure of ourselves. When you speak, speak with confidence. When you go into a boardroom, take up as much space as possible (like men do), instead of minimizing your space at the table. Stand tall. Simply drop the apologies and qualifiers when you speak and others will see you as authoritative and confident. Know what you are saying and say it with strength.

- Handle Conflict with Grace: Instead of engaging in conflict or avoiding it, learn to communicate. Acknowledge the conflict and ask, "So how do we move past this?" Don't engage in or allow personal attacks; keep things professional. Don't email when you are angry and don't read emotion or tone into texts, emails, or directives. Don't hold a grudge; once the conflict is over, shake hands, hold your head high, and get back to work.

In the next chapter, we'll discuss how to get very clear on what you want and why you want it.

# CHAPTER 4

*Getting Clear on What You Want and Why*

I'm guessing you wouldn't have picked up this book unless you wanted to get ahead in your career. If you are looking to improve yourself and be the best version of yourself, then you deserve to achieve success and all that comes with it.

Now, I can give you every tip and trick in the trade on how to get ahead in business. If you use it, you *may* succeed. Then again, you may not succeed. What is the difference between achieving success and not? Why do some people keep getting ahead in their careers and become leaders, while others continually struggle and slog through the drudgery aimlessly, day in and day out? They drift in and out of trying to move their career forward without actually achieving anything.

Let me ask you a question. If you knew your specific ideals for lifelong fulfillment were at the end of a 1700-mile road trip, would you go without knowing the exact destination? I doubt it.

What do most successful leaders do consistently that helps them get ahead, stay ahead and be fulfilled? The answer is simple: Goal Setting.

Goals are powerful. They make the imaginary real. They drive us to succeed. They focus our attention on getting what we want. They give us a framework and a road map for developing our vision of who we want to be and what we want to have. Goals motivate us to turn our vision into reality. They are a powerful process for imagining our ideal future and developing a plan to get there.

The process of goal setting helps you choose your direction in life. It puts you in the driver's seat, as opposed to letting life lead you astray. By knowing exactly what you want to achieve in your career, you'll know what activities and efforts you need to focus on. You'll also be able to easily spot distractions and correct your course if things go in the wrong direction.

**Why Goal-Setting Is Important**

Setting goals gives you long-term vision. It is a powerful tool to focus your activities and help organize your time and resources to make the most out of your life. You've heard that goal setting is important. You have likely even tried to set goals for yourself, or followed some sort of program to do so. Why is this important? Why should we bother?

Goals give you focus. They force you to only undertake the activities that move you closer to the desired goal you want to achieve. The more you do things that allow you to achieve your goals, the closer you will get to the desired finish line. Conversely, goals allow you to identify those efforts that are not moving you closer to your goals. By letting go of the activities that move you away from your goals, you actually become more efficient in achieving them.

Goals help you stay motivated. Let's face it: the day-to-day work environment can get you down from time to time. Goals help you break out of that. They help you see the amazing future that's out there for you. By seeing the potential, you can get (and stay!) excited about your future. And it goes without saying that if you're excited about your future, you are more likely to act and do things that will lead you to your future goals.

Goals reinforce your confidence. One of the biggest challenges women face in male-dominated fields is their perceptions about their own worthiness for achieving success. Writing down your goals switches something on in your brain and helps you develop *certainty* that they can be achieved. The more certainty you have, the more confident you will be. The more confident you are, the higher the likelihood that you will succeed.

Goals help you achieve more. Goal-setting triggers new behaviors that focus your resources towards fulfillment of those goals. The more you achieve smaller goals, the more confident and better you feel. This then gives you a sense of self-mastery and motivates you to undertake more activities that lead you to your goals. The more you achieve, the more confident you feel in your achievements and then the more you achieve after that. This self-fulfilling circle leads most people to achieve more than their original goals envisioned.

Study after study has shown that when people set goals, something in the brain is triggered toward achievement of these goals. That's why the vast majority of corporations set annual goals for themselves. It works.

So, why should you set goals for your personal career? Same reason. It works.

## My Personal Experience with Goal Setting

Early in my career, I sat at the kitchen table every Sunday with my husband. We would go through our goals together. We started by outlining where we wanted to be in 10 years. We had goals like, Be Mortgage Free, Pay off the Line of Credit, Be President of a Corporation, Achieve a Project Management Professional designation. We threw in everything we could think of so we could get started. We even started to think about what kind of house we wanted to live in and whether we wanted a swimming pool (yes!).

After we knew where we wanted to go, we thought about what we needed to do to get there. That's when we came up with our 5-year goals that would have to be achieved before we could achieve our 10-year goals. Our 5-year goals were more like:

- Pay off the line of credit
- Have only $100,000 due on our mortgage
- Be the VP of Business Development at a large firm
- Etc.

Great! So we had our 5 year objectives. That was still a long way off though, and it didn't seem like the objectives were all that achievable. So, we took things one step further. We wrote down our 1 year goals. One year is pretty short in the grand scheme of things, and things you put in your 1 year goals are imminently achievable.

Some of our 1 year goals were:

- Pay $XX off in our line of credit.
- Pay $YX off on our mortgage.
- Decide what neighborhood we wanted to live in and how many bedrooms we want in our house.
- Get the manager job opening that had come up at work.
- Do a "lunch n learn" for my colleagues about some lesson I learned in the company that would raise my profile at work.
- Write a thought piece on the direction of the company and share it with colleagues.
- Deliver our projects on-time and on-schedule.

Then, the *pièce de résistance*. . . every Sunday night after dinner, we would plop our kids in front of the TV and review our 1 year goals. We would go through each one and set up a list of activities we would need to do *that week* in order to achieve the goals.

Something powerful and amazing started to happen.

We actually started to achieve our goals. My husband applied for a high-paying job at a telecom company and got it! I started to step up at work by offering to lead on a few special projects that would go to the executives and writing thought pieces for the company. I also started to ask higher level people in my company out for lunch to get their views on how I could be more successful at work.

The people I met for lunch became my biggest advocates in the company. When there was a shiny new high profile project, and they needed a project proposal specialist, they called me. They didn't call me because they knew I was brilliant. They called me because I stepped up and actively asked their opinions. Just by doing this alone, I ended up with a slew of colleagues in higher positions that were my biggest cheerleaders and who helped me further my career.

Goal setting works for everyone. The more I was reminded weekly of my 10 year, 5 year and 1 year goals, the more I worked toward them every day. My efforts eventually seemed to snowball and take on a life of their own.

**Visualize Yourself 10 Years into the Future**

So, how do you get started?

Think about this: Where do you want to be in 10 years? If 10 years is too abstract to think about, then think about all the things you want to achieve in life. Make a list of between 5 and 8 goals. You can either use a spreadsheet to create a table, or you can use the tables at the end of this chapter.

In the first column, please write all the things you want in life. Go crazy! You want to be the president of your own company, *Bam!* Put it in there. You want to have $5 million in the bank to travel to Tahiti whenever you want? *Bam!* Put it in there. You want to lead a team of creative, aspiring people that propel your company forward? *Bam!* Put it in there. You want a handsome butler to bring you coffee in the morning and lay out your clothes for the day . . . you get what I'm saying?

Take note of this: Ensure your goals are "SMART." SMART stands for Specific, Measurable, Achievable, Realistic and Timebound. It's the difference between stating, "I want to be rich" and "I want to have a job that pays me $1 million annually, after tax." Make sure your goals are objective and measurable. The more specific and "SMART" they are, the higher the likelihood that your goals will be achieved.

The next step makes the key difference between normal goal setting and actually achieving the result, in my humble opinion. In the column next to each goal, I want you to write down *why* you want this goal achieved. It's the *why* that leads us to pursue the goals, not just the goals themselves. The *whys* can include any number of possible reasons:

- I want to feel recognized for my contributions to the company's success.
- If I had a bigger house, I would have more room to do the things I enjoy.
- If I had a swimming pool, my kids would be happier and healthier.
- I would feel valued and loved.
- I can never choose what to wear in the morning and a butler would help me be more efficient . . . You get the idea.

Literally thousands of goal setting techniques and apps are much more sophisticated than what I have come up with. I encourage you to look around and find some great resources for own personal goal setting. Myself, I like to keep things simple and straightforward. If I can't do it on a spreadsheet, then I probably won't do it.

Here's an example of what my own personal 10 Year Goal Setting Activity looks like:

## 10 Year Goal Setting Activity

| # | SMART Goals *(Specific, Measurable, Achievable, Realistic and Timebound)* | I Want to Achieve This Because |
|---|---|---|
| 1 | To be an executive in my company making at least $1,000,000 per year in salary and bonuses. | • I want to influence the company's direction. <br> • My skills and ideas will increase the company's revenues by 30%. <br> • If I make that much money, I can send my kids to the best schools and buy a swimming pool. |
| 2 | To be a thought leader in my industry that is paid to speak at a minimum of 3 conferences per year. | • I have interesting ideas that greatly benefit others. <br> • I love public speaking, and it makes me happy. <br> • I want recognition and to be thought of as a rock star in my industry. |
| 3 | To successfully complete a Master's Degree in Business Administration. | • I want the external credentials to give me credibility in the job market. <br> • I will get a significant raise with this degree in hand. |

Now that you've set your long-term goals, think about the things you have to achieve in 5 years to make your long-term goals happen.

Draw the same table. This time, do it for 5 years. I want you to think about what you need to happen in 5 years in order to get closer to your long-term goals. Some examples may include:

- Be the Director of Market Development for my company.
- Start my own business and achieve revenues of $100,000 in the first year.

- Get a Master's Degree in business administration.
- Have $60,000 in savings to start my own business.

The thing here is that we want to make these 5 year goals specific. Here is where you start to focus on making your goals SMART.

An example of a 5-Year Goal Setting Activity may look like this:

### 5-Year Goal Setting Activity

| # | SMART Goals (Specific, Measurable, Achievable, Realistic and Timebound) | I Want to Achieve This Because |
|---|---|---|
| 1 | I want to be promoted to Director of Market Development by the time I am 30 years old, with an annual salary of at least $150,000. | • I deserve to be promoted based on my hard work and killer ideas. • The higher salary would let me save for a family trip to Switzerland. |
| 2 | To enroll in an Executive Master's Degree program in Business Administration by 2022. | • I want to add credibility to my resume. • I will feel accomplished, and other people will have greater respect for my skills. |
| 3 | To attend a minimum of 5 networking events per year in my field. | • Meeting more people in my field will help me get ahead. • I love meeting people and getting to know them. • The more business relationships I make, the more cheerleaders I will have to help me in my career. |

Finally, I want you to write your 1-Year goals. What can you achieve in the next year that will move you closer to your goals? Do you want . . .

- To take one course in business management at a local college that will help you to start your own business, and graduate with a minimum grade of 80%?
- To pay $10,000 towards your Line of Credit?
- To write a thought piece on a key challenge in your industry for publication in a trade magazine?

Here is where you are getting very specific. The more specific you can be, the better. And again, these goals absolutely must be SMART in nature. Once you have finished writing your goals, I want you to write the reasons why you want to achieve them like we did before.

The difference with the 1-Year Goal Setting Activity is that you can now start to jot down some actions that you can take today or over the next few weeks to turn your goals into realities.

Write a list of at least three things you can do to get yourself started today. This is your Action Plan. Do you need to enroll in a course? Do you need to sign up for a networking event? Whatever it is, I want you to gain momentum and the only way of doing that is to undertake activities to get you to where you want to go.

Here's an example of a 1-Year Goal Setting Activity:

### 1-Year Goal Setting Activity

| # | SMART Goals (Specific, Measurable, Achievable, Realistic and Timebound) | I Want to Achieve This Because |
|---|---|---|
| 1 | To be promoted to Manager of Market Development with an annual salary of at least $110,000. | • I work hard and deserve to be promoted.<br>• I have a lot to contribute to the company.<br>• I'm a great manager of people. |

| 2 | To save $15,000 that will be used for my Master of Business Administration program. | • I will need to pay for my new degree.<br>• I am worth investing in. |
|---|---|---|
| 3 | To enhance my social media profile by filling in my LinkedIn account and having people write testimonials and endorse me. | • If I have an awesome LinkedIn profile with endorsements, people will think more highly of me.<br>• A public profile showing my capabilities with testimonials will add credibility to me personally if I go for a promotion or apply for a new job. |
| **Action Plan to Make My Goals a Reality** | | |
| 1 | Ask 3 business colleagues to write a testimonial on my LinkedIn page. | |
| 2 | Volunteer for a new project at work. | |
| 3 | Set up an automatic savings program through my bank. | |
| 4 | Sign up for a webinar on leadership. | |

No matter what your goals are, there are three easy ways to get started. You may want to include these in your Action Plan:

1. *Go to a networking event and talk to people.* It can be *any* networking event. Even during social restrictions, there are numerous opportunities to engage in online, virtual platforms where you can meet new people in your field. If you don't know of any, do some research about networking events in your area in your field. Look up the local chamber of commerce or board of trade in your area. Seek receptions or conferences that interest you. It doesn't even have to be anything in your field. I want you to go out there and start talking to people—both men and women. Successful, savvy business women know how to feel comfortable talking to people. It's a muscle that we are going to build slowly. And set a timeline for yourself. Like, in 2 weeks, you will go to a networking event and talk to at least 5 people that you don't know. Talk about

your work. Talk about whatever you're passionate about. Talk about your dog. Whatever it is, just do it. We need to build up our networking muscles.

2. The second thing I want you to do is to *get a mentor* (more about that in the next few chapters). Start by identifying one person that can help you in your career. Maybe ask them for a virtual or face-to-face coffee to get their insights.

3. The third thing is *talk to your boss*. Find out what she or he wants and expects of you. Get clarity on your weaknesses so you can come up with a plan to overcome them. I don't know a single boss who wouldn't want an employee to step up like that.

So now you have your goals all set. Will they change? Likely. But at least now you have a roadmap for your life. Congratulations! That's something to celebrate! Now go out and complete one of the actions you listed.

In the next chapter, we'll talk about how you take these goals and turn them into reality by knowing your stuff.

# CHAPTER 5

## *Do Your Homework . . . Like, Really Know Your Stuff*

In February 2008, my stress levels had gone through the roof.

I was assigned to a special team of 20 people at work. Our mission was to put forward a proposal to the government for a $5 billion project. This project was the company's number one priority. In fact, the future of the company was at stake. If we won this project, we would all get to keep our jobs. If we didn't . . . well, I didn't want to think about that.

Our competition was fierce. Two other major global players were aggressively trying to displace us. These competitors dwarfed us in every way. They were enormous. They sold more projects than we did. They were able to offer things that we couldn't.

My job was to analyze the competitors to see how we could make our offer even better than theirs. While others in the project team focused on outlining the benefits of our technology in the proposal, I went about trying to learn everything I could about our competitors including what would likely be in their bids.

The biggest competitor was a French company. They were huge. They had lots of different businesses, and they could use some of them to offer things that we couldn't. I spent days pouring over all the information I could find on them. I looked at how their previous projects were bid. I looked

48

at all their business lines. I started to put together a picture of the things they were likely to include in their proposal. After weeks of searching, I figured out that the competitor was going to include free fuel contracts as a "sweetener" in their bids—something we could not offer.

I approached the proposal team and showed them what I found. In preparation for this meeting, I had spoken to some project team members about what we could offer to match our competitors' "bid sweetener." As I spoke to the proposal team, I recommended that we include a free multi-year service contract as part of our bid in order to put our proposal on equal footing with our competitors. The proposal team agreed, and the service contract was included in our bid.

We won. The multi-year service contract that I recommended for the bid was cited as one of the reasons the government chose us over the French company.

**Facts Matter**

Nothing is more critical in business than knowing your stuff. Success is not for suckers. As a woman in a male-dominated field, you have to know all the nitty gritty details to get ahead. Why? Because our credibility is constantly questioned. We have to be prepared. The best way to be prepared is to gather all the facts and evidence you can to support what you are trying to do.

In Her Words . . .

I was the Project Manager in the field on a project that had multiple trade subcontractors working for our firm. As day one began, I sat in my truck (no logo) and watched as my project team gathered, one labeled vehicle at a time. As they congregated drinking coffee and eating their breakfast, waiting for the Project Manager to arrive, I watched. Everyone appeared to have a comradery and some certainly knew one another from previous working experiences (*Note: observation is important*). I wanted to maintain that dynamic.

I exited my truck walking towards the group. Eyes flitted towards me, down to the ground, back to others in the group and then back at me. I had no idea what they were thinking. I picked the few smiling guys in the group, looked them in the eyes and I introduced myself as the Project Manager.

I gave a daily rundown, sub appointments scheduled for Day 1 and some basic expectations (*Note: always be prepared*). As the day went on most of the workers were readily open to the meetings and were prepared to have meaningful interaction regarding their work (*Note: I was building rapport, setting standards, respecting their knowledge and letting them tell me how they understood their job. I also demonstrated to them I understood their scope of work*).

The painter was the exception. He was going to challenge me every step of the way. I did not flinch or even try to debate with him. He was a handful. There seemed to be a discrepancy over the color of the paint he had in his truck, he was insistent he was correct (*it was not per the corporate specification in my opinion*). I let him run with his opinion, as he had primer work to do first. At lunchtime, I brought him the paint spec while no one was around, and asked him to review it just in case we did have a misunderstanding. I asked him to decide for himself and proceed accordingly. I reminded him respectfully that his boss would be paying for any rework required and I didn't want him to have any issues with his boss.

He left the site that afternoon, did not tell me anything and the next morning, he began painting with the acceptable paint per the specification. I never brought it up again and neither did he. I still laugh about this experience. I went on to work with this same guy on several other projects. He was no longer a handful.

I found that the more prepared I was, the more respect and compliance I got from the guys around me.

*Yolanda Troxell, MBA. Sector: Fire Protection Systems for Power Plants*

Men and women have different ways of communicating. In male-dominated industries, the focus is most often on the facts. Put another way, in order to be influential in these industries, we have to be clear on the quantitative, objective and measurable reasons why we should pursue a certain course of action.

In the early days of my career, I would go up to one of my bosses and say something like, "We should consider doing *this*." Whatever *this* was. From my perspective, I was fishing for his views and perspectives on whatever I was trying to convince him of. I wanted to get a feel for whether I should pursue that course of action. I had no evidence that what I was considering would work. I just wanted to find out his views.

Big mistake. He started to ask me questions about what it would involve, how many people he would have to devote to it, what the budget would be and what could we expect in terms of results. He was certainly within his rights to ask these questions. The problem was, I had no answers for him. I responded that I would have to do some research and get back to him. By that time, he had already dismissed my idea because I had not come to him with the information he needed to make a decision. He was right.

I started to realize that men and women handle new ideas differently. When I'm with my girlfriends, one of us will sometimes bring up a business idea. We will then talk about it together. Each person will bring an idea to the table on how to make it better. Each will contribute their unique expertise until we have the whole thing flushed out. After roughly an hour of talking about it, we will likely have a full business plan with roles defined, a budget, a schedule, and a marketing plan. It is an approach that is collaborative and cooperative.

Things don't work that way in businesses that are dominantly male. Men tend to focus on fixing things instead of empathizing. When you come to them with a problem, and you don't have a full solution, there is an assumption that you are looking for their help solving it. If you float an idea, they expect that they need to play a role in finding the solution.

Men also tend to gravitate toward hierarchy and competition. Within the hierarchy, everyone has a role to play. The lower tiers feed information to the upper tiers. The upper tiers make the decisions and then flow it back to the lower tiers to implement.

If I want to get a new idea adopted, I've learned that I have to approach others with the entire solution, not just a concept. I have to have all the reasons why it is needed. I need to have all my evidence and facts straight, with references. I have to know exactly what we can expect in terms of budget and schedule. And, I have to base my recommendations on case studies where the same idea was successfully implemented elsewhere.

**Do Your Homework**

When you are trying to pitch a new idea, there is no substitution for doing your homework. You need to know all the facts and figures before you approach others.

Let's use a case study to demonstrate this.

Suppose you find out that there's a robot arm that can do a certain job much more accurately and cheaper than it is done now. You think it would be a great idea if your company bought this robot arm and used it for the hard-to-do tasks. First, you research the types of robot arms on the market. You make a list of the different types, their features and their costs.

Then, you need to go deeper and understand the technology of the robot. Is it hydraulic? What are the electricity requirements? How long does it take to set up? What are the software requirements? Is it compatible with your software? If not, what do you need to do to make it compatible. You document your research. Then, you need to do a cost analysis. How many hours of work will your shiny, new robot arm save? How long until you can recoup your initial investment? Then, you'll need to do a benefits analysis. What are the direct and indirect benefits that the robot arm will give the company? Will it not only do things faster, but also increase the amount of business? How much extra business will this robot arm allow you to take on? How much more money is that for the company? Finally, you'll want to put together case studies on how companies similar to yours succeeded with the robot arm and what kind of results they got.

Yes, we need to get to that level of detail. And that's before we have even approached anyone to see if it's a good idea. Going through this exercise does two things. First, it ensures you are prepared to handle any related question. When you are prepared, you immediately have credibility. People take you seriously when they see you've done your homework. The second benefit is that you'll quickly discover whether the idea is worth pursuing. If you start your research and find out that the robot arm is completely incompatible with your company's current operations, then you'll know from the start it's a no-go. This way, you know whether to pursue something before approaching your boss. You've saved face and you've saved time.

Once you have a solution with all the facts and evidence to back it up, then you need to sell others on the idea.

**Be Prepared**

The flipside of knowing your stuff is being prepared. So often, I see both men and women make this mistake. They will go into a meeting without an agenda, without knowledge of the items to be discussed, and without understanding the perspectives of others in the room. This is especially problematic when you are trying to move something forward in the business.

When I was selling nuclear reactors for a living (yes, you read that right), I was asked to put a business plan together for a certain technology that we were developing. I had done my research and diligently looked into each market. I had all the facts and analysis in place. The forecast I put forward was aggressive but achievable. All the i's had been dotted and t's crossed.

The business plan was going to be discussed and approved at an upcoming meeting. I knew my colleagues did not have time to read it before the meeting. They were busy running their own departments. While they were interested in the business plan, it was highly unlikely that they would have a deep understanding of it. Hence, I knew I would be walking in cold—*never* a good idea.

To increase my chances of success, I decided to set up one-on-one meetings with each participant. When I met with each colleague, I gave them an overview of the business plan. I answered their questions. Then, I asked what they thought of it and whether they had recommendations to improve it. Some suggested tweaks to the business plan. Many had no comment, yet said that they appreciated being given the heads-up about this matter in advance of the meeting.

By doing my round of meeting with everyone, I not only got their input regarding the business plan, but I also drastically increased my chances of success. The other great thing about doing this was that whatever objections they had to my business plan, they told me privately in advance instead of at the meeting. If I had waited until the meeting, their objections may have ruined my chances by showing their disapproval in front of everyone.

When the meeting finally took place, we sailed through the business plan and approved it without many changes.

The more prepared you are in advance, the more successful you are likely to be. This can apply to anything from meetings to proposals to your annual performance reviews.

How do you ensure you are well prepared? Here are some ideas:

- Research, research, research. Find out everything you can about the topic at hand. Get all the information and evidence in order. Make sure you know more about the topic than your colleagues.

- Review your facts. Is there anything that would or could contradict what you are trying to put forward? If there is, can you come up with a response in advance?

- Think of other objections to your ideas in advance. Imagine what your colleagues might say in response to some of your ideas. Does the company lack financial resources to implement your idea? Will the changes result in a different environment that will make your colleagues uncomfortable? Then, do some research and come up with pre-prepared responses to those imaginary (but likely) objections.

- Talk to people in advance. Get to know their thoughts. They may have recommendations about your idea that make it even better. Use their ideas as much as possible. The more they feel like they have contributed, the more they are likely to accept it.

Preparation and knowing your facts does wonders for getting ahead in male-dominated fields.

**Stay on Top in Your Field**

Another important part of doing your homework is staying on top of new developments in your industry. Not only will it increase your knowledge, but it will increase your credibility when discussing business with your colleagues. You will be able to showcase your knowledge about new technologies and market trends and developments that can seriously change your business. The benefits are massive.

Staying ahead in your field can be done in multiple ways. I recommend a broad approach. Are there industry associations you can join? Are there conferences you can attend? Are there lectures or events where highly respected people in your field will be speaking? Try to get out there as much as possible to connect with people and learn.

Even if your boss doesn't want to commit the funds to send you to conferences, you can still stay on top in your field. Early in my career, I offered to take notes at conferences for the organizers in return for a free pass. It worked most of the time. Or, I would find a way to attend an event outside of work hours. Lots of events put on by local Chambers of Commerce are relatively inexpensive to attend and are often held during lunch, in the evenings or on weekends.

Another key benefit of staying on top of information in your field is the opportunity to meet people outside of your immediate work environment. Networking is a powerful tool for getting ahead in your career. The more people you meet, the more you learn. People I met at conferences ended up helping me the most in my career. Being friendly and talking to people enabled me to find new career opportunities, be asked to join international committees, get promoted and earn more money. The more you put your face out there, the more you will succeed merely through the expansion of your network.

Here are some ways to continually stay up-to-date in your field:

- Attend seminars on your area of work—there are literally thousands of webinars and seminars every day on a wide variety of topics. Learn about them and attend the ones that are most relevant to your career. Talk to many random people. Pass out business cards to everyone. You never know whom you'll meet and who will help you in your career. Ask lots of questions. Even during social restrictions, there are lots of online opportunities to learn new things and meet new people.

- Read trade magazines—Often, new ideas appear here first. From new technology ideas to company announcements, trade magazines/e-mags are often a great resource for finding out what's new in your sector. They also include analyses on the pros and cons of new technologies or ideas, giving you additional knowledge about both sides. Another great thing about trade magazines is that the articles are often written by key people in your industry.

Get to know their names and their companies' names. Get to know what they do. If you are ever in a bind and need some hard-to-get information, you'll know where to look.

- Join an industry association—I cannot recommend this enough to women in male-dominated industries. Industry Associations are a breeding ground for new ideas and innovations. When you need a resource or information, industry associations should be your first contact. If they don't know the answer, they will likely know whom to contact to get that answer. Also, the people you meet at industry associations are full of knowledge and love to share if you step up and ask them.

- Find out what your competition is doing. If someone else is getting great results, find out what they are doing. Your competitors are also your source for new developments in your field. Have they put in place a new system that is helping them win more bids? Find out what that is and how you can incorporate it in your company. Or, if you're competing with another company on a bid, do some research and find out what will likely be in their bid so that you can make your bid better.

Be hungry for information throughout your career. The knowledge and connections you gain will work miracles for your future success.

In the next chapter, we will talk about how the new people you meet from networking can develop into mentors who can help you in your career.

# CHAPTER 6

## *Mentors - Your Secret to Getting Ahead*

I had gotten to the point in my career where I began to think about starting my own business. The rat race of the big corporate world was getting to me, and I felt I needed to make a major move to validate my skills and see if I had what it took to go it on my own.

The year was 2008. A global recession was happening, and businesses were failing left, right and center. I was nervous. Should I stay where I was, or should I make the leap into entrepreneurship? Did I have what it took to be successful on my own? Should I partner with an older, white male who had more creditability than I? I had so many questions.

At this time I called someone I had worked with in the past. Jacqui was older than I and was an executive at one of the big four consulting companies. Years earlier, I remembered that she had said I could ask her for advice whenever I needed to. My fingers were trembling as I dialed her number. Would she remember me? Would she help? Did she want to meet for lunch? The answer to all three was *yes*.

We went to a fancy downtown restaurant that was full of big wigs. As soon as I finished telling her my idea, she looked at me and slapped the table.

"Rosemary," she started, "You don't need an older white man to guide you or help you get credibility. You already have what it takes. You have way more experience than the people you are mentioning, and I have no doubt that if you start this business, you will be successful."

Jacqui was a true mentor. And she was right. I did have what it takes. Within a week of starting my new business, I was referred to McKinsey & Company who awarded my first contract—three weeks of work for a very lucrative amount of money based on my specialized knowledge and ability to find out pricing information.

Would I have made the decision to start my own business without Jacqui's advice? I don't know. What I do know is that her support and confidence in me, as well as the support of my many other mentors, propelled me to embrace the future and believe in myself.

## What Is a Mentor and Why Are They Important?

Put simply, a mentor is anyone who helps you along your career path. They are your sounding board, your sanity check, your advisor and your friend. They support your decisions and help you get the resources you need to move up the career ladder.

Does one person fit neatly into the box of a mentor? Of course not. Realistically, no one person can meet all your needs in a mentor. Hence, the reason for having many mentors.

In Her Words . . .

Look for role models, male or female, who have experienced and accomplished things you admire, aspire to doing and/or wish you'd done. Connect with them. Ask them to be a mentor. You'll be surprised how flattered they will be and how freely helpful they will be in most cases. Anyone who turns you down is not somebody you want to emulate anyway. However, be selective about what you want to learn. You will quickly discover you do not want to emulate all that your mentor does. You will often find your Emotional Quotient (EQ) is quite different, so you want to emulate hard skills rather than soft skills. Or you will find you want to emulate someone's soft skills, but their hard skills aren't similar or equal to yours.

> For instance, I have had Executive Assistants and Human Resource managers that I learned piles from about how to fairly and kindly handle difficult conversations with colleagues, staff and even bosses/Boards.
>
> *Carolyn Preston, CEO. Sector: Oil & Gas*

Mentors come in many shapes and sizes. It can be your boss, your boss's boss, your colleague, a person in another company, or a person in the industry. Really anyone. To succeed as a woman in a male-dominated business, you need a variety of mentors--both male and female--at different levels and with different perspectives.

Early in my career, I had quite a few mentors. My boss was keen to get me involved in extra projects. My boss's boss and I had had some interactions. He also recommended my name when it came to new projects and promotions. The Director of Communications took me under her wing and helped me draft a report. Some colleagues that I worked with at other companies and even in government also played a role in mentoring me and helping me succeed. Each brought a different perspective, and each one played a key role in helping me navigate the corporate world.

In Her Words . . .

After graduating with a Chemical Engineering degree, I accepted a position in the nuclear industry as a safety analyst. Upon establishing myself in nuclear safety and licensing work, I decided I wanted to move into management. I had a strong track record of success managing project teams. I approached my manager at the time to discuss the path towards management. My manager sighed, and then proceeded to tell me that to succeed as a manager, I needed to be aggressive and "nice" people could not lead. He went on to point out that I had young children and motherhood is demanding, so I might not want to commit the amount of time that is needed to be a manager. The conversation lasted about fifteen minutes and impacted me greatly.

It certainly set me back, but it also made me question my own capability. I decided to hold off on pursuing management – maybe a technical role was best. The hardest part for me at that stage in my career, is that I did not have a female role model to turn to for advice.

About one year after that discussion, a mentor did enter my life. While it was not another woman, it was a leader who was extremely well-respected, quite senior in our industry and someone whom I would not describe as aggressive. Watching him, for the first time, I saw the leader I wanted to be. That was when I realized that in a male-dominated profession, I would need male leaders to pull me up. As the years went on, I continued to grow my set of mentors and added some tremendous women to that list. In seeing some strong leadership examples, I was able to go after positions I wanted, knowing that other people like me had succeeded in those roles.

Today, I am honored to have mentored some incredible people, both men and women. The key messages I pass to them from my own experience are simple:

1) Find a role model that exemplifies the leadership qualities you want to have and build a relationship with them. Ask them questions and get their advice.
2) Surround yourself by people that will support you and challenge you to be better. Avoid the naysayers.
3) Do not assume the smartest person in the room knows everything you know. We all bring different pieces to the conversation. It's about bringing diverse views forward.
4) If the opportunity doesn't exist, create it yourself.

*Rachna Clavero, Executive. Sector: Nuclear Energy*

As my career began to take off and I became an entrepreneur, my network of mentors grew. It started to include more and more people from other companies, from think tanks, and from industry associations. I learned that I could find mentors among the executives of other companies and significantly improve my chances for success.

But how did I get so many mentors? And why did they decide to help me?

By now, you have already completed the activity of reprogramming your beliefs. The first step to getting a mentor is to believe in yourself. No one will believe in you if you don't first believe in yourself.

**Activity:**

Write a list of the reasons why someone should mentor you. It can include big reasons and little reasons. You need to be clear on the value you provide and how you can move things forward. Some items on my list included the following:

- Working hard. I will keep working until late at night to get things done.
- Paying attention to detail. When I'm putting an event together, I make sure that everything has been thought of and considered to make the event a success.
- Being a great collaborator and team player. I know how to take a group of people and make them cooperate to achieve a certain goal.
- Being enthusiastic and eager to learn and get ahead.

**The Psychology of Getting a Mentor**

Why should people help you? If you completed the activity above, you have already outlined a number of reasons. Is it enough? Unfortunately, no. Mentorship is actually a two-way street. People don't always help you just because you ask. Often, there has to be something in it for them.

For people to help you, you need to understand the psychology of getting a mentor. A lot of it boils down to the theory of reciprocity which states that if you do a favor for someone, they will likely do a favor for you in return. It's human nature.

So, to find a mentor, you need to think about what is in it for them. How do they get ahead by helping you? Do they end up looking better to their bosses because you did a good job? Do you enhance their customer relationships? Will your help them get that promotion they are looking for? Or, can you write a letter of recommendation for someone applying for a job?

The point is that you need to be altruistic before you can expect help. Examples from my own career include the following:

My boss trusted me to put together a conference on the Environment in Trade Finance, where the president of our company would attend. I worked with other departments, including Environmental Review and Communications, to organize the conference. I was well prepared for everything that could go wrong. The conference had an international attendance list, and I made sure that all attendees' needs were met, including overcoming language challenges and food preferences. The content of the conference was carefully put together to promote discussion. When the conference finally started, the president got up to give the opening remarks. As he stepped down, he pulled my boss aside and told him what a wonderful conference it was and that he had truly earned the promotion to vice president.

Making my boss look like a superstar and get a promotion made him a mentor for life. He acknowledged to the team that I was the reason for the conference's success and from that point on, he helped me get ahead by taking me with him as he moved up the company ladder. Suddenly, I found myself being trusted with more responsibility, being questioned less, and actually getting a promotion to where I had a small team of my own.

That one act of making my boss look good to *his* boss yielded years of dividends in terms of moving my career ahead in a way that I could not have enjoyed without someone ensuring I was continually moving up the career ladder.

A less intense example involves my early days as a consultant. At the time, I went to many conferences trying to get clients. I would outline the value of having an outsourced business development team and how it could cut costs and raise revenues. At the time, I had been trying to land a major customer in the energy sector. As the conference day came to a close, I asked people from that company if they wanted to meet up for dinner.

When we got to the restaurant, we saw that most of the tables were taken and that the people I had asked for dinner had no room at their table. There was no room at the table for the vice president of operations, director of business development and me. I suggested that we take another table closer to the back and that dinner was on me for the three of us. During dinner, the vice president (Frank) outlined some of his challenges in business development. I listened carefully, asked many questions and then gave him some preliminary thoughts (for free no less!) on how to gain revenues in certain markets.

Two years later, Frank had moved on to become president of another company. I guess he was impressed with what I had said two years earlier, because he called from his new company and asked me to be his business development consultant for the next six months. From then on, when I needed help with a problem or wanted to meet someone he already had a connection with, Frank was there to help with advice or an introduction to a connection that could be helpful for me. This person became not only my mentor, but my friend for life.

A key thing in finding a mentor is asking yourself: *What can you do for them?* The theory of reciprocity says that when you do a favor for someone, they feel obligated to help you in return, whether it is required or not. Most people will. Again, though, it is up to you to make the initial move and step up to help them.

### How to Find Mentors

Where do you find mentors, you may ask. My answer is: everywhere. While that's not a very clear answer, my point is that you need to get out there to find mentors. People will not come to you and help you out of the blue. It is your job to expand your network as broadly as possible to find people whom you can assist and who can assist you.

Here are some ideas for where to find mentors:

- **The company you work in.** People in your company are your best source for learning how to get ahead at that company. Is there someone you are impressed with? Can you ask them out for coffee or lunch? Can you ask them about their careers and how to get where they are now? Could you ask for their advice on how someone like you could get ahead? Of course you can! Don't feel like you need to stick with people in your team or your department. Reach out to people in other teams and functions. Reach out to your boss. Reach out to the nerd in accounting. You may learn a few things along the way. Not everyone is going to be helpful. But, in the process of reaching out to many people in your company, you not only get your name around but you learn more about how things work and hence how to get ahead.

- **Industry associations.** If you haven't already figured it out, I absolutely love industry associations. They are an efficient way of getting to know a lot of people at a lot of levels in a lot of companies. Better yet, industry associations tend to be the breeding ground for new ideas and developments. Attend as many industry associations as possible. Talk to random people. Introduce yourself to as many people as possible. Ask them about themselves and how they got ahead. Offer to take them out for coffee or lunch and a chat. By doing this, you will get known in your industry and be recognized as a leader--whether you are or not--by the sheer fact that people know you. Volunteer for their committees. Offer a helping hand at organizing conferences. There are so many ways to get involved. The most important advice I can give you is to talk to random strangers. You never know whom you will bump into.

I attended one industry association event for construction in the power generation industry. I was one of only three women in the audience in a room of over two hundred men. While I was nervous, I made an attempt to speak to as many people as possible. After a tiring two days, it was time to leave. I still hadn't gotten what I wanted out of the conference, so as I was leaving, I decided to talk to one more person who was seated in the hallway. I approached him and asked how he liked the conference. We started talking and it turned out he was the vice president of a major multi-national company that was looking for business development advisors. Bam! I had made a connection. I then treated this person to lunch and he became my mentor in the construction of power plants.

One last word on industry associations . . . many women's books on success tell us to focus on women-based organizations. While these are phenomenal places to find mentors, and I have used them extensively, it would be wrong of me to say that exclusively focusing on women's organizations will get you ahead in male-dominated sectors. I have observed that you don't get ahead if you focus only on female-dominated associations. In order to succeed in these unique sectors, it is important to join both women's and other industrial associations.

You want to get ahead in male-dominated fields. By excluding involvement in associations that are for both sexes, you are cutting yourself off from more than 75% of the decision-makers of your industry. From a purely statistical perspective, that is craziness. Of course, women's organizations have a lot to offer in terms of career development and mentorship, but they shouldn't be the only organizations you belong to and are involved in.

- **Conferences**. A wonderful place to meet mentors is at conferences. People are generally happier and friendlier at conferences. Why? They are away from the challenges of work and they are filled with interesting people. Walk around the trade show floors, talk to people, introduce yourself to the person in front of you at the coffee or lunch line. Listen to the speakers and ask them questions afterwards. Ask a variety of people if they want to meet up for dinner after the conference.

**How to Get the Most Out of Your Mentors**

Now that you have a wide variety of mentors in your network, how do you use them to get ahead in your career? While finding mentors will naturally give you more recognition and credibility within your industry, it is important to know how and when to draw on your mentors for advice.

## Be Selective

No one wants to be hounded 24/7 with questions on how to get ahead. Try to be selective regarding the people you approach and the questions you ask. I heard a great quote once: "Don't go looking for limes in a shoe store." In the same sense, do not ask people for advice if they haven't experienced something similar. If they have, offer to meet. After first asking how they are doing, outline your problem and ask what they would do in your situation. Again, we are focusing on *them*. Make them look like the superstar by saying things like, "You have so much experience in this area, and I knew you would be the right person to talk to." By making them feel good about themselves, they are more likely to help you with your situation. Don't be afraid to ask them to connect you with other people who have similar challenges and solutions.

## Spend Time with Them

Maintain your network of mentors by maintaining regular contact. I know this may seem obvious. Sometimes we forget that we have people we can reach out to.

On a regular basis, give your mentor a call to see how they are doing. Better yet, have a regular scheduled meeting with them. It could be over coffee or lunch. There doesn't have to be a reason to get together. Just by spending time with them and getting to know them, you'll have a better sense of what they do and how they can help you, or--for that matter--how you can help them. Either way, they will appreciate your stepping up and reaching out and will be more likely to help you.

I have one friend (we are actually mentoring each other), who calls me once a month to catch up and bounce ideas around. I love it! I love the attention and her friendly tone. She always makes me feel great, and I in turn do whatever I can to help in her career, whether it be writing a letter of recommendation or introducing her to someone who can help her.

Being in contact with your mentors helps you remain in their thoughts. It also ensures that they are getting to know you and your needs. Most of all, it helps build friendship and trust. Ultimately, your mentors should become your friends. Once that happens, helping each other becomes a natural extension of your relationship.

## Outline Your Goals and Get Your Mentors' Feedback

It would be impossible for your mentors to help you if they didn't know the direction you are going. You have hopefully by now written out your 10 year, 5 year and 1 year goals. Show them to your mentor. Discuss them at length. Get their feedback on your goals and what you need to do to accomplish them. Ask them what they think you should be doing to achieve them.

You'll be surprised at the amount of feedback and help you'll get on your goals. Perhaps they can put you in touch with others who can help you.

## Be Prepared

Over time, you will develop rapport with your mentors and figure out exactly how they can help you. When you are ready to discuss an idea for getting ahead and are looking for their feedback, show up prepared. That means: Do your homework, research the idea and be ready to answer questions they may have. They are likely busy people, like yourself. If you have all the information ready before you get their opinion, the meeting will go much more smoothly.

Quite a few years ago, I was meeting with one of my mentors. He was a government employee who ran a certain section of the electricity system. I wanted to get his feedback on a certain idea, so I asked him out for lunch to pitch the idea. Once we ordered our meals, I started to discuss the idea and ask for his input. My idea was in the infancy stage. I wanted to know if it was feasible before I invested more time. It turns out, this was the wrong approach. He asked question after question about the underlying technology I was suggesting, the time for development, and the cost. I knew none of the answers. I was so embarrassed. "Call me when you figure out the details," he said as we were leaving. I felt so bad. Not only had I wasted his time, but I had also put a dent into my reputation for being prepared. I left the luncheon with my tail between my legs.

The next time we met, I was fully prepared with all the facts and figures. I had put together some costing information from estimates I found online. I had conducted research into the different technologies and ranked them according to my opinion of their likelihood for commercialization. When we had lunch the second time, I laid out the presentation I had developed. He was impressed. He gave me suggestions on how to pitch the idea to his superiors, including one recommendation that made the entire perspective more appealing. That one recommendation resulted in creating a graph that clarified the problem I was trying to address.

Based on his suggestions, I went back to the drawing board and re-worked my idea. The graph I developed showed the supply and demand of the entire electricity system and how we needed to plan now for the future. The message couldn't be more clear. I used that information to pitch the idea to my mentor's bosses. It worked. A year later, I saw my graph in a government document that was circulated to all electricity companies in the region.

It pays to be prepared, especially with your mentors. Use their valuable time respectfully by having all the information they will need in advance.

In the next chapter, we will explore what to say when you don't know the answers to their questions.

# CHAPTER 7
## *Faking It Until You Make It*

Do you notice how your male colleagues always look confident? They seem to strut around with their heads held high. They seem to have the answer to every question. They assume that success will be theirs, and lo and behold, it is.

There is so much to learn from our fabulous male colleagues. Seriously. Imagine if you had 100% confidence in your abilities and everything you tried worked out. You'd be a freaking rock star! Instead of being intimidated by this confidence, let's try to replicate it using *their* techniques.

Maybe you don't yet have the confidence you desire. Maybe you've been told so many times that you are not good enough that you are starting to believe it. While I call *baloney* on that one, there are ways you can fake being confident until you actually are confident. This also applies to being knowledgeable, experienced and skilled.

In order to fake leadership, recognition and success until you make it, you have to be intensely curious. It is like being Sherlock Holmes. If you observe carefully, men use a variety of techniques when they are unsure of themselves to make them appear confident.

So what are these techniques? I'm glad you asked. Some were learned through observation. Some were told to me by friends. And while this is not an expansive list of techniques to exhibit success and confidence, it's a good start. The rest will be up to you to observe how men in your company/industry behave and to replicate the behavior until you achieve the desired level of confidence.

**Technique #1: Decide how you want to show up every day.**

Quite a few years ago, I had to attend a boring lunch reception and speech for work. I didn't want to be there. There was so much work waiting for me back at the office and so many calls to be made. I was feeling tired and overwhelmed, and the last thing I wanted was to be social with a bunch of strangers that had—at best--only a tangential connection to my work.

When I entered the room, the woman at the front desk handed me a slip of paper that contained the number for the table where I would sit. When I approached the table, it was full. Only one space was left beside an older gentleman, so I sat down.

The man looked at me, and to my surprise he said, "Well, hello there! We've been waiting for you to join us!" *That was nice,* I thought. I made my introductions and sat down to eat. No sooner had I put a spoonful of soup in my mouth than the man turned to me again and said, "I want to hear all about you. Tell me all about your life and your work." He paused. "Oh, I'm sorry I asked you a question when you just took a bite. I'll wait then. But I know it's going to be fabulous!"

Now, that really changed my attitude. Suddenly, I perked up. This stranger was interested in what I had to say! I found myself talking about my work and my family. Then, he shared information about himself and his work. We had a good laugh about so-called "Sin Stocks" that included companies that sold racy products and services, and which never went down in a recession. By the end of lunch, I was engaged, appreciative and energized. And it had to do with how this person decided to show up.

Deciding how to show up at work is a key technique I've learned about being a successful leader. You may have had a bad day or a fight with your partner the night before. You may be frustrated and tired and sick of constantly having to prove yourself. You may complain about the work you're doing or the people you're not getting along with. You may look

71

tired and stressed and unhappy. Well, guess what? If you show up to work that way, people are going to treat you as someone who is frustrated, tired and stressed.

What if you decide to show up present, fully alert and engaged? What if you decide to show up imagining that you are the leader that everyone is relying on? What if you decide to show up ready to listen to your colleagues and ask meaningful questions? Would you be perceived differently at work? *You betcha!*

The way we decide to show up at work, regardless of how we feel internally, determines how others perceive us. It can be the difference between being seen as a leader or being seen as a liability.

The next time you walk into work, ask yourself: *How will I show up today?*

Are you going to hold your head high? Are you going to be alert and attentive to your colleagues? Are you going to be enthusiastic about your work? These are traits of a leader, wouldn't you agree? If you're exhibiting your best self when you show up to work, you'll be perceived as your best self.

So, go out there and show up as a leader. You have nothing to lose.

**Technique #2: Answer a question with a question.**

Men are amazing at handling the unknown. In the face of a challenge, they will step up to the plate and show how important they are, even when they have no clue what is being talked about!

How do they do this? One simple technique is to *answer a question with a question.* The question you ask needs to be focused on the individual who asked the question. Your response question should make the person feel important and not reveal that you don't know the answer.

When I was still working for a big corporation, I remember attending an event where an older man walked up to my boss (another older male colleague) and asked what he thought of a recent corporate development. Now, I knew for a fact that my boss had no idea what he was talking about. Moreover, he had no idea how to respond to the person's question. As I stood there wondering what he would say, I watched in amazement as my boss looked meaningfully at the other man, waited a moment and said, "Well, that is something. What do *you* think about it?" The other man ended up talking for ten minutes about his thoughts, giving my boss time to learn about the issue and form an opinion. After the other person spoke for a while, my boss repeated what the other man had said and asked another question, "What do you think this means for the company over the next year?" In a matter of ten minutes, my boss had gotten the other guy to outline the entire story and state his opinion. All the while, my boss made it seem like he knew exactly what was being talked about and was interested in the other person's opinion. Brilliant!

This technique can be used widely in your career. When someone asks you something that you are not entirely sure of, it is better to ask questions than to say something irrelevant and--perhaps--be thought a fool.

Here are some ideas of what to ask when you are in a bind:

- What is *your* opinion?
- How did you come across this information?
- Does this align with our strategic plan / business goals?
- How can this improve our business?
- What does your boss think of it?
- How do we get buy in from others--*or*--how do we get this idea off the table?
- What implications do you think this will have?

Asking a question with a question gives you time to respond. It also helps clarify the original question so that you have a better basis on which to establish your answer.

**Technique #3: Develop a strategy for answering a question when you don't know the answer.**

It's always tough when you get asked a question and you don't know the answer. On one hand, you don't want to seem like you don't know your stuff. On the other hand, you want to make sure your answer satisfies the questioner. Sometimes, answering with a question isn't appropriate and we have to take a different approach. You don't want to dance around the question or make yourself look like a fool. So, what do you do?

Having been in this situation more times than I can count, I can tell you there is no easy answer. There are times when I have blurted out an answer without thinking, and there are times when I've taken a calculated approach to ensure I came out on top. I recommend having a toolbox of strategies to use for different situations.

There are several strategies for when you need to answer a question and you don't know the answer. Here are some ideas:

- Get clarification - It is entirely appropriate to ask for clarification to the question if you are not sure what is being asked. By asking the person to clarify, you are getting more information. This information may lead you to realize you actually do have an answer. Or, it may lead you to know for sure that you don't have an answer. Seeking clarification shows that you are interested in the person's question and are taking time to understand where they are coming from.

- Empathize – Sometimes, people are asking you a question because they want you to agree with them on an issue that is causing them anxiety or anger. Everyone needs a shoulder to lean on when they feel emotional. Another useful tactic that I have found is to not answer. Instead, use words that are empathetic and helpful. You could try saying something like: "That must be frustrating," or "I can see where you're coming from." They will likely keep talking and value you for listening instead of providing an opinion.

- Postpone your Answer – Sometimes, you are stuck in a situation where you have no idea what the questioner is asking. You may be put on the spot. You may not have even heard of the issue. Or, it may be so controversial that you need more time to collect the facts. Alternatively, you may want to offer a solid answer, and you need to do research before saying something that could be incorrect. There is absolutely nothing wrong with stating that you don't have the information they are looking for at the moment, and that you will get back to them. Then, collect the facts and follow up and give them the answer in a reasonable timeframe. *You don't have to have all the information in the world all the time.* Postponing your answer shows that you are not willing to provide information in an area where you are not yet informed. People will respect you for wanting to provide correct information, as long as you follow up.

**Technique #4: Imagine yourself as a queen.**

I'm being a bit facetious here, but this technique works. Early in my career, I was told that I wasn't being listened to because I was young. This hit me hard. I didn't know what to do about it. It's not like I could change my age.

I asked a colleague if any young woman in the company had risen to be a director. He mentioned a woman named Diane. Now, I didn't know Diane, although I had certainly heard of her. She was a powerful woman heading up the strategic planning division, and she was a special advisor to the president of the company. Boy, was I intimidated to approach her.

I finally picked up the phone and asked her to meet, saying I wanted to get insight about how she handled the people I worked with when she was in my position. To my surprise, she was eager to meet with me.

"To get everyone's respect around the room at such a young age," she started, "I imagined that I was the Queen of Sheba. I sat around the boardroom table with my back straight and my head held high. I carefully listened to what people were saying and only expressed an opinion or asked a question if it significantly added to what was being said around the room. I imagined that I was in charge of everyone, and they all started to act like I was."

This was amazing to me. Could I fake being a successful leader even if I wasn't one? I was about to find out. At the time, the movie *Star Wars: Episode 1 – The Phantom Menace* had come out. The character Queen Amidala was my inspiration. She was a young queen who ruled an entire planet with grace and elegance. I studied how she walked, stood and spoke in the movie and tried to replicate it. I spoke slowly and clearly in a low voice.

At the next project meeting, I entered as Queen Amidala (at least in my head). I sat straighter, elongated my neck and spoke slowly and carefully. My colleagues, I noticed, paid more attention to me. My words weren't wasted as I only spoke when I had something important to say. At the end of the meeting, I acted as if I ruled the planet by asking what actions would arise from the meeting and who would be responsible for them . . . you know, for my notes. From then on, when I went into a boardroom, I adopted that strategy. People seemed to respect me and listen to me and within less than a year, I got my promotion.

**Technique 4: Take up space.**

Have you ever noticed the difference between men and women in a boardroom?

Picture this: A man walks into a boardroom. He chooses a chair and lays all his things on the table in front of him so that he takes up the maximum possible space. His computer may be placed in front of him, but back a bit. His notebook is about a foot away from his laptop on his right. He then flings his phone to the left side of him and it ends up on the table about two feet away. Pens and other accessories get strewn about haphazardly. His stuff goes over to take up table space in front of the other chairs. As he sits in his seat, he leans back, crossing one leg over the other knee. He then puts his arm out to the side and rests it on the back of the next chair over, emphasizing how much space he is taking up.

Next, a woman walks into the same boardroom. She chooses a chair near the end and places her laptop neatly in front of her. Her notebook, pen, phone and other accoutrements are placed very close to the laptop, respectfully ensuring there is plenty of space at the table for other people and their things. Then, she sits close to the table with her hands folded in front of her. She's taking up as little space as possible to be respectful.

Do you see the difference in the two approaches? The man claims his territory and superiority by expanding his presence, while the woman (in trying to be courteous) minimizes her occupation of space.

In doing this, the woman subconsciously is exhibiting her core belief that she does not fit in and doesn't deserve to be there. Without knowing it, she is showing others that her presence is "less than" compared to her male colleagues, even though this is not her intention.

The lesson here is: Take up space. Put your things around you. Lean back. Make yourself look as comfortable as possible in the space you are taking up. Believe in yourself and your right to be in the room as much as anyone.

**Technique #5: Dress the part.**

Men are so lucky. There are few options regarding how they dress and present themselves. They have a few suits, a few pair of nice shoes, ties, that's it. Women, on the other hand, have a multitude of styles to choose from, not to mention hair, nails, makeup, etc. It takes much more work to look presentable as a woman.

In male-dominated fields, this technique is crucially important. To succeed in these sectors, your colleagues need to feel that you are part of the team and that includes the way you dress and look.

Don't get me wrong; it has been my life's goal to one day dye my hair pink, or even purple. But I know that wouldn't fly with my male colleagues and I wouldn't be taken seriously at work.

Everyone has their own style. It's important to be yourself. At the same time, to succeed, you may want to observe how women in your industry dress, especially if they are leaders. Do they typically wear suits? Are their clothes colorful, or do they prefer the basic black and gray? Are there ways you can spruce up your navy suit to add understated elegance? Whatever your style, remember to observe how other successful women in your field dress and try to emulate that.

## Technique #6: Learn to play golf.

Don't laugh. They say business is where you talk about golf and golfing is where you talk about business. Where can you better get to know executives than by spending an entire day of camaraderie playing golf? Golf is the game of business, and we are in the game of getting ahead in business.

The great news is that you don't have to be good! Loads of people will try to help you along the way and give you tips and tricks. The point is, you're trying. You are showing up and saying to the world, "I want to succeed!" You're making the effort to be a part of the business world. And the dividends will pay enormously.

---

In Her Words…

My recommended way to succeed in a male dominated industry is learn how to golf. Don't be afraid to join your company's golf league or even start one yourself. "Golf League" is the code word for getting out of work early on a Thursday.

Pro-tip: most industry conferences include a golf day before or during a conference, which means you can spend the day outside networking, instead of inside for 8 hours of technical sessions. Don't let the term "Golf Tournament" at an industry conference intimidate you. Typically, golf tournaments during conferences are "best ball" and you'll be paired with 3 other golfers. Everyone shoots, but you just keep the ball closest to the hole.

---

It's acceptable to not be that great at first and you'll improve over time. Golf gives you four hours to network in a more casual, private setting.

Golf has given me job opportunities, sales, friendships, and great memories. My favorite golf experience was playing with the Chief Executive Officer and Chief Financial Officer of my company at a famous course in England – all expenses paid. I'm proud to say I didn't get fired because I wasn't a golf pro, but now I consider these Executives to be close colleagues of mine.

*Submitted by: Erin Wehlage, Director of Business Development. Sector: Software Technology.*

Faking it until you make it is not about being someone you are not. It is actually about being your best self. It is about showing the world the confidence you are building and ensuring you get noticed. Showing up as a leader every day and taking up space ensures you will be taken seriously, now and for the long run. It significantly increases your chances of success in business.

Now that you look and act the part (and have signed up for golf lessons!), we are going to show you how to take credit for your accomplishments!

# CHAPTER 8

## *Taking Credit for Your Accomplishments (You Go Girl!)*

We put in an incredible amount of work to succeed. We work long hours, toil harder than others, and ensure everyone is on board. And when we finally succeed and accomplish something great, what do we tend to do? We stay quiet.

Men, on the other hand, are phenomenal at taking credit for their accomplishments. Let's look at how men take credit. If a male colleague is leading a team that achieved success, he will shout it from the rooftops. He will tell everyone about it. He will talk to his colleagues about how he did this, and he will portray confidence and determination along the way.

In a study recently published in the *Personality and Social Psychology Bulletin*, researchers Michelle C. Haynes and Madeline E. Heilman conducted a series of studies that revealed women were unlikely to take credit for their role in group work in a mixed-gender setting unless their roles were explicitly clear to outsiders.[5]

So, what happens when we receive a compliment or achieve a success? We tend to downplay it or give the credit to the team who helped accomplish the goal, instead of accepting accountability and kudos for the accomplishment.

The tendency manifests itself in many ways, and we often see it played out when things like this are said: "The team really did all of the work." And while it may be true that you have a good team and that others contributed to the success, we savvy business women need to accept our role in the success.

Why do we hesitate to accept credit for our accomplishments?

Many highly successful women often talk about impostor syndrome, where they don't feel they are worthy or deserve success. In their study called, *"Advancing the Future of Women in Business: A KPMG Women's Leadership Summit Report,*[6]*"* the big consulting firm KPMG studied this phenomenon. They defined imposter syndrome as the inability to believe your success is deserved as a result of your hard work and the fact you possess distinct skills, capabilities and experiences. It somehow seems that no matter how accomplished we are, we tend not to give ourselves the credit we deserve. We struggle with feelings of inadequacy and low self-confidence.

Women tend to downplay their accomplishments for many reasons; *some* women do this because they:

- don't want to be disingenuous when other people also contributed to the success.
- think it should be obvious that they were the successful ones in the accomplishment.
- fear seeming egotistical and annoying.
- fear being perceived as "aggressive."
- have been socialized to downplay or refute compliments.

If we are to be successful, we have to overcome imposter syndrome. We have to change from the inside out. This change is not only for ourselves, but for the women who will come after us. We need to re-program ourselves and show others a good example of how to take credit for our accomplishments.

I wish it were as easy as flipping a switch. It's not. Like a muscle, we need to start small and keep building and exercising every day to get over our lack of self-confidence. Slowly but surely, we can develop ways to ensure that we feel valued and deserve our success.

There are many ways to get started. The ideas put forth in this chapter are by no means exhaustive. I have found that these ideas work for me. Hopefully, they will work for you, too.

**Find Your Cheerleaders.**

The number one way I have found to develop confidence and believe in my accomplishments is to be told about them by others. For some reason, I can tell myself I'm great at something a million times and not truly believe it. When someone else tells me the exact same thing, I gush. I'm honored. More importantly, I truly end up believing what they say about me. Then, I think, *Wow . . . if only I could see myself the way others do.* Eventually, I did. The more I reached out to others and built relationships based on trust, the more others started to point out how great my accomplishments were. Based on that, I started to gain the confidence I sorely needed. I started to believe in myself. Taking credit for my work after that came easily.

Start with something you may are already great at. Are you good at building relationships? Then, build relationships with your peers. Build relationships with others in your industry. Try connecting with people where you see a mutual benefit. Does someone need help acquiring information? Offer to do it for them. Does someone need help meeting someone you know? Make an introduction. The more you help others, the more they will in turn help you and become your cheerleaders. You will start to be seen as a savvy businesswoman and an influencer. Suddenly, the people you reached out to help will become your biggest allies.

I have a friend named Gale whom I met at a conference. She was one of those up and comers that was noticed right away. We sat on a committee together and found we shared many ideas. The day after the committee meeting, I ran into her and she asked me out for lunch. We quickly became fast friends. She recommended me for a higher position on the committee based on my ideas and willingness to volunteer. She always told me how much she appreciated my work and how great I was. She then introduced me to a group of people that I became friends with. The more I spent time with them and talked about new ideas, the more great things they had to say about me. I was overwhelmed by their confidence in me. They respected me. They looked forward to hearing about my ideas and work. In short, they became my cheerleaders.

I took the confidence I earned from my cheerleaders back to my day job. What a difference it made! Suddenly, I knew I was an accomplished person *because a bunch of other people told me so.* And I believed them. I started to speak up at meetings. I held my head high. I was less intimidated by the "old white guys" who thought they knew everything. Moreover, my work colleagues were impressed by the caliber of people I now called my friends. These friends happened to work in some of the biggest companies in the field. Knowing I could call on them and get the information I needed was an ego boost and it impressed my peers. I received a new level of respect that made me feel confident about taking credit for my accomplishments. People started to view me as a mover and shaker, and in turn I believed that about myself.

You too can build your cheerleading squad. The beauty is that you may already be good at making friends and building relationships. Work with that. Reach out to people and offer to help them. Can you take someone you admire out for lunch? Or coffee? Can you make a point of congratulating a colleague for a job well done? Your cheerleading squad is there, ready to help. You just need to reach out.

**Change Your Language.**

Focusing on our language is a way to gain confidence and take credit for our work. Language shapes our thoughts. If we use language that unintentionally diminishes our place in this world, we will feel diminished. The opposite is true, too. If we want to be seen and recognized as successful leaders in male-dominated fields, we have to change the way we talk to ourselves. We have to train ourselves to accept successes and compliments.

In Her Words…

I received a phone call from the YWCA CEO (Heather) who left a message on my machine. It said something like, "Hey Brenda, call us. This is the Toronto YWCA and I want to talk to you." The first thing I thought was, "I didn't apply to the YWCA for a job. Why is she calling me?" Well, she called again and said, "Brenda, you have won the Women of Distinction for your work with the Canadian Women's Hockey League." I was like, "Wow, that is such a huge honor."

When you are given the award at a celebration gala, you get to make a three-minute speech. Not a seven minute one. They give you three minutes and say make it work. And, of course, my name being Andress, I get to go first. So, I walk up to the stage to receive the award and make my speech. In my mind, I am thinking, "I have three minutes and I want to make an impact, but more importantly I want to say something that's going to change my life." Because again, I go back to: the person who can make a difference or a change in our ourselves or the world is me and you.

I walked up to the podium and man, I have got to tell you… this is one time I was about to give a speech and I was nervous. I knew that what I was about to say could be controversial, and yet I knew I was going to say it because it is what I genuinely believed.

So, I took a deep breath and looked out into the crowd and I said, "Thank you for the honor and for this wonderful award of the YWCA Women of Distinction, and I just want to tell you that *I am deserving of it and I'm worthy of it.*"

There was a silence that hung in the air and for a brief moment. 1,000 women in the same room were quiet. And I was like, "Oh my gosh." And then I continued and specifically said, "Why? Because I think as women, we do not believe that we are worthy and deserving of so many things: in our lives, in our jobs, in our relationships, and in the opportunity to make change. And tonight, at this event, I want to add one more to my list. I want to tell you that I belong."

After that award, I grew in believing that I belonged at the tables I chose to sit at. Today with the women's sports organization I run, *SheIS,* I am saying that we belong as women in the sports world. We can make a difference with the simplicity of believing we are worthy, deserving and that we belong.

*Brenda Andress is the founder and president, SheIS, and founding commissioner of the Canadian Women's Hockey League*

When people give us compliments about our successes, let's take ownership. Instead of saying things like:

*"We got lucky."*

*"It was a team effort."*

*"It was nothing."*

We can start saying things like:

*"I'm proud of the role I had in achieving this."*

*"Thank you. I put in a lot of hard work and it was worth it to be successful."*

*"It feels great to have achieved this!"*

And when you want to talk to people about your accomplishments, tell them! Be simple and straightforward. Be specific. You will come across as genuine when you use quantifiable, objective and measurable evidence. And you will feel more comfortable.

Some examples of this could be:

*"I helped reduce expenses 5% last year by implementing new project management tools in my department."*

*"I was the lead proposal writer for the $1 million account my company just landed."*

*"I led my team to increase revenues by 50% in the aerospace sector in the last two years."*

The more specific you are, the more comfortable you will be in telling your story. When you can quantify and qualify your accomplishments, they become real and believable, both to others and yourself.

If someone congratulates you on a true team effort, here are ways you can respond to realize your share of the credit:

*"The team did a fabulous job. I'm so pleased that my role as the project manager ensured the results."*

*"Thank you. The team did a wonderful job, and the idea I had about X really helped us snag the final win."*

Always emphasize your accomplishments within the kudos that your team gets. After all, without you, the result would not have been the same.

**Share Your Story.**

One thing that always bothered me was figuring out how to showcase my accomplishments without sounding like I was bragging and full of myself. Pumping yourself up in front of others can be awkward at first. You want to acknowledge your work and get others to acknowledge it, but you don't want to seem arrogant. Despite the awkwardness, getting credit for your work feels amazing. When you feel amazing about your work, you tend to do better work and achieve more. I asked myself: "How could I let people know how great I am without coming off as being ego-centric?"

What worked for me was telling stories that aimed to help others. If there is a challenge around the boardroom table or if someone comes to you for advice, share your story. Paint a picture of the situation you were in and how you handled it. Make sure your intention to help is clear from the very beginning.

Examples in this context are great. Let's say you and your colleagues are sitting around a boardroom table and someone raises the issue of how to deal with a competitor. You can say something like, "Dealing with competitors is a key challenge we need to face. When I wrote the business plan for this product, I found that our competitors were strong in marketing, but their price points were too high. We want to get ahead of the competitors and gain market share, right? My experience in analyzing the competitors for the business plan led me to believe that they were not going to lower their prices even with increased competition. If we came in at an introductory price that was appealing to customers, I believe we could win up to 20% market share within the first year. That would give us a chance to have a foothold in the market before we increased our prices and made more profit."

In this example, you clearly outlined that you are the authority on this topic since you wrote the business plan. You are not bragging that you wrote the business plan. You are suggesting how your experience with the business plan can help the people around the table make more profit.

Ultimately, you want to educate people on the steps you took to be successful, and inspire them to be successful as well. If stories about your accomplishments come from a place of helping others, they will be valued, and you will be recognized as an influencer.

**Keep Others Informed of Your Contributions.**

If we are passive about letting others know our accomplishments, we risk letting others take credit for our work.

There are times when you are absolutely within your rights to share your accomplishments with others. Maybe you won a big project at work. Maybe you increased sales in your department by 20% per year for the last 3 years. Instead of staying quiet about it, try talking to people about it. Don't just share the results of what you accomplished. Share the journey.

Share all the ups and downs and challenges you faced and the steps you took to overcome them.

As long as you are sharing the journey with them, it will come across as sincere and helpful instead of bragging. Be specific about the details. The more specific we are, the more real the story will come across.

Another way to keep others informed about your contributions is to make presentations. Your presentations should be aimed at sharing lessons learned. I love presentations because they give you a platform to share accomplishments with others without coming across as egotistical.

Suppose you worked on a project that involved a number of challenges. The end result is that the project came together at the end in a successful way. Can you put together a lessons learned presentation and host a Lunch n Learn to share your learnings with your colleagues? You bet you can. People love hearing about how others handled tough situations and overcame them. They *want* to hear your stories. It gives them new information about how to succeed when dealing with similar situations. On top of that, you come off as a superstar.

**Take on Your Own Projects.**

Sometimes, life gives us opportunities to shine. Does a new project need managing? Is there a risky situation where the upside is a raise and a promotion? Does a major improvement need to be made, and yet no one wants to take it on? Can you ask your boss to give you projects that you can own? Jump on those opportunities.

Stepping up and taking the reins on a project is a great way to prove your worth. You will be able to demonstrate your worth at several places during the process. First, you can put together a project team with you as a leader, demonstrating your management skills. Second, you can show your organizational skills as you build and implement a project plan. Third, you can look for feedback from your male colleagues along the way so that they have a stake in your success. Fourth, you can provide progress reports that demonstrate the skills you've gained, the results you achieved and how you brought things together. Finally, if the result is positive, you have a concrete example of your success to share with others. You'll be in the forefront of your own success. Once the project is finished, everyone will recognize that you were the one that pulled it together, especially if you take credit for that accomplishment and show others how it can help them.

**Work Your Accomplishments into Everyday Conversations.**

Business is no place for wallflowers. Your male colleagues take every chance to tell you about their work and their results. Sometimes it seems that every conversation is about accomplishments. Instead of rolling your eyes and changing the subject, join in! Be part of the conversation and talk about your own work.

You can subtly let people know your worth through everyday conversations. For instance, someone will ask, "How's your day going?"

You can respond with: "Great. I just completed a major project on implementing X software throughout the company, and it has already resulted in Y." Practice letting people know about your accomplishments. The more you do, the more comfortable you will feel.

You could also ask a question that implicitly shows off your work. For instance, you can say, "Hey, did you see the latest numbers from finance? It looks like my initiative on cost-cutting measures is working."

The more you do this, the more your colleagues will come to recognize how you have actively contributed to the company's success. You've worked so hard to get where you are. You have a lot to be proud of. Grab a megaphone. Shout it from the rooftops. Step up and get heard.

In the next chapter, we'll talk more about empowerment and what to do when uncomfortable situations get in your way.

# CHAPTER 9

## *The Chapter that No One Wants to Talk About (How to deal with Sexual Harassment)*

---

NOTE TO READERS: Please know that this chapter does *not* reflect the attitudes and behaviors of all men. All men are different. Most men do not sexually harass women in the workplace. This chapter intends to refer only to *the cohort of* men who continue to sexually harass women in male-dominated fields. This chapter is meant as a guide to help women who face this behavior. Anyone experiencing such behavior that threatens their career, needs to contact the appropriate authorities.

---

As I write this chapter, I feel sad and disappointed that any women's career success manual needs to include this topic. It is unfortunate. The reality is that in male-dominated fields, instances of sexual harassment are significantly more prevalent than in industries that are more equal from a gender perspective. Harassment flourishes in these environments because in the past there has been a climate of tolerance and a culture of silence.[7]

According to McKinsey's "2018 Women in the Workplace[8]" study, 35% of women have experienced some form of sexual harassment over the course of their careers. This percentage jumps to 45% of women working in technical fields, which are male-dominated. Others estimate that the real number is between 40% and 80% in this field. It is often the reason many women shy away from male-dominated sectors. It is also why women grow tired of being exposed to harassment whereas their counterparts in other fields are less affected.

The good news is that things are getting better. The #MeToo movement and other successful anti-sexual harassment campaigns have successfully exposed this unacceptable phenomenon. Increasingly, workplaces are more serious about inappropriate behavior. Whistleblowers are getting the protections that they so desperately need. Complaints are being taken more seriously and human resources departments are stepping up.

The sad truth is . . . we have a long way to go. Try Googling "Sexual Harassment in Male-Dominated Fields." You'll find countless articles, research and documentation about the continuing challenge that this phenomenon poses for women.

In 2018, my life partner Brent and I were at a business conference for the power sector in Amelia Island. After a long day of lectures, panel discussions and networking, a party was organized by a sponsor company. Brent and I decided to attend. I didn't have time to change, so I wore my business suit for the party (*Sidenote: it's sad that I even have to mention what I was wearing*). We moseyed up to the bar and ordered drinks. While waiting for our drinks, Brent mentioned he needed to go to the bathroom. I stayed at the bar waiting for our drinks. Just as he left the reception room, I felt someone come up from behind and start humping me! I was shocked! I turned around and was face to face with the CEO of an engineering company that I had been trying to pitch for some business. The man put his knuckles in his mouth and inhaled deeply. "God, I just have to tell you how sexy you are," he said, as he ogled me.

As shocked as I was, I kept my cool. This was a well-known and respected person in my field. I had to keep it together and deal with the situation in a professional and sane manner, while not creating waves that could destroy my business reputation.

"Thank you for your compliment," I responded. "My boyfriend is on his way back now, and I'm very committed to him. I'd like you to respect that."

I'm not sure that was the best thing to say. Should I have been more assertive and said his behavior was obnoxious and I should report him to the conference organizers? At the time, I was so taken aback that I couldn't conceive an appropriate response.

I wonder how many women have had such a crazy encounter in a male-dominated field. Let me tell you—things like this happen. And they continue to happen. In any other field, the police would have been called. In male-dominated fields, however, people often turn a blind eye. And while things are changing due to the #MeToo movement, there is a general sense that if people acknowledge that it happens, they no longer need to do anything about it. And so it continues.

### What Does Sexual Harassment in Male-Dominated Fields Look Like?

Sexual harassment takes many forms: The range goes from asking for a sexual favor to making comments about a woman's appearance. Obviously sexual harassment hurts women's careers and inhibits women from succeeding. Let's unpack that a bit.

A favor for a favor:

Sexual harassment can take the form of a negotiation. If you do something for me, I'll do something for you. When someone explicitly asks for a sexual favor in order to get a job, keep a job, or get a promotion, that's sexual harassment. We are being told in no uncertain terms that in order to get ahead, we have to service men sexually. You can imagine how a woman would be shocked to tears when faced with this. If she does do it (*not* recommended), she faces the guilt of using her body to get ahead. If she doesn't, she gets passed up for promotion or whatever the favor is. Either way, her career suffers a serious setback.

Creating an uncomfortable work environment:

Most sexual harassment does not involve sexual requests. Instead, direct or indirect comments about a woman put her in an uncomfortable position. It can involve commenting on a woman's appearance, making vulgar jokes about women, staring at women's body parts, or simply making sexist comments. Other times, technical equipment or tools are referred to in sexual terms.

Often, this "locker-room talk" is seen as no big deal. However, in the workplace, this talk creates a hostile work environment. We are being told that we do not belong because of our gender. We are made to feel unwelcome and unfit to do our jobs. Not only does it have an impact on our well-being, but it also can have a nasty effect on productivity and work engagement. Ignoring this behavior and getting on with work is difficult.

Now, I am by no means an expert on *why* this happens. Some people say that it's because women have not traditionally been in male-dominated fields, so they are not taken seriously and are seen as eye candy. Others say that creating equality in this regard is very difficult because men have been raised to either take care of women or use them. If they aren't taking care of them, e.g. their wife or daughter, they feel some sort of unendorsed and ungiving right to use them for pleasure.

Whatever the case, the only thing we can control is how we respond.

In Her Words . . .

I was working for a consulting firm at the time and we were heading to this conference in Las Vegas to provide lead generation services and bring foreign direct investment to the area.

One of the after parties was at the Grand Bellagio. I went there with a friend that I had made from the trip (another business man).

We decided to go out to the terrace overlooking the fountains. (This is where everyone was smoking and it was obvious at this point that everyone had a bit to drink)

My friend started talking to this group of men. They clearly had ignored the fact that I was there. My friend then introduced me.

When he introduced me, one of the gentlemen said, "You are a consultant, eh?" He then went on to say, "Ha ha. How old are you? Pitch me beautiful."

So I did, and when I was done, he said, "Wow, you are really smart for your age. I would hire you,"

I then looked at him and said, "I wouldn't let you, because I would never work for a jerk like you." (Rude I know, but I had absolutely no time for being treated with such disrespect and I likely wouldn't see this man again.)

The truth is, you will meet some jerks that are stuck in their ways! But this world is changing for the better and focusing on women and what we bring to the table. Deal with the jerks and hold your head high. For every jerk out there, there are 10 gentlemen that will help you to be the successful business woman you want to be.

*Jenna Shaw, Business Development Manager. Sector: Construction*

Plain Ol' Sexual Come-ons

Don't ask me why, but for some reason there are men out there that think they can approach a woman sexually in a work environment. Unwanted sexual attention takes many forms. It can be an inappropriate text or picture sent by a male colleague. It can include sending suggestive letters or emails. Or, at worst, it can involve inappropriate touching. Regardless of the form, sexual come-ons that occur in male-dominated businesses create a toxic work environment. It makes the workplace an anxiety-ridden and uncomfortable place for women.

## Factors that Contribute to Sexual Harassment

While I'm not a psychologist, numerous articles provide indications as to why some men in male-dominated fields conduct themselves inappropriately with women. There is no excuse for this behavior. However, it is interesting to learn about the research concerning why sexual harassment occurs.

Proving their Masculinity

As I mentioned earlier, competition is the norm in male-dominated fields. Some men continuously feel the need to prove their masculinity in a number of ways. One of these ways is to make women feel uncomfortable and thereby reinforce women's lower status. This behavior makes a man appear to be the alpha male in the group.

Another finding in my research led me to believe that some men harass women sexually as a way to shut women out of the group, thereby reinforcing the masculine identity and proving their manhood. The thinking here, as I understand it, is that the women in the group are taking the jobs that "should" in their minds go to men. By undermining women sexually, men explicitly let them know that they do not belong.

Using it to Fit In

In other instances, some men make vulgar jokes about women or sexually harass women to feel like "one of the guys." For some reason, some men feel that by putting women down, they fit in better with the higher-level of men in their corporate environment.

This type of group mentality is heightened in male-dominated businesses. For instance, if there is a group of alpha men, the beta men will do everything they can to fit in. This includes a variety of sexual harassment behaviors that help prove themselves equal to the men in the group.

## Sexual Harassment Is the Norm in Some Industries

It is sad to say, but in some industries women make up only 5-10% of the workforce, and sexual harassment has become the norm. These workplaces are characterized as "hyper-masculine," where the culture is aggressive and competitive, and away from the public eye. Many in these fields may not see the behavior as sexual harassment because it is so common. Women in these environments are a fraction of the workforce. They can be subjected to constant vulgar chatter, come-ons, and other forms of sexual harassment.

## Maintaining Professionalism Amid Pandemonium

How can we handle these situations with grace and elegance, while remaining professional and being taken seriously? It's a tricky balance. There is no one right answer. Certainly, various strategies can be used to address these situations. Many women I've spoken to have offered their insights on this topic. Here are some options to help you through this situation:

### a.) Be Clear About Your Hard No.

When these sticky situations happen, it is critical to maintain composure. It is so easy to get disgusted, angry, hurt and to feel belittled. If you need to walk out, go to the bathroom and have a good cry, do that. You have every right to feel the emotions you face when confronted with this type of situation. But showing emotion in front of your male colleagues is— in their eyes--a sign of weakness. You need to find a way to push these emotions aside for later and address the situation at hand.

Be clear that what was said/done was inappropriate. Assert that you are not interested. Sometimes, it's as easy as saying, "No. That is inappropriate." You could even be more assertive and say, "Absolutely not." Or "Hard No."

Anything wishy-washy can and may be used as an excuse for the behavior to continue. It may even be seen as playing hard to get, or an invitation for the same continued behavior.

Some other things you could say are:

*"That kind of talk is inappropriate. Please stop it."*

*"Do not give me more compliments. I don't like it."*

*"I don't want to be talked to that way."*

*"Please stop or I will report you to Human Resources."*

The clearer you are in saying *no* and asking them to stop, the better chance you have of getting out of the situation. Be stone faced. Don't waiver. Speak clearly and assertively.

### b.) Document It

While you are deciding how to handle the matter, it's always a good idea to document the instance of sexual harassment. Maybe keep a logbook or a file of what happened, and make sure this file is in a safe place. You may wish to keep a copy at home in case something happens to your computer at work. Include the date, time, location, name of the person, their title and exactly what was said or done. Keep track of the behavior through your logbook over a period of time.

If you end up reporting the behavior, you will have a detailed and fact-based account of what happened. Having a document or account of the precise events will provide credibility.

You may end up doing nothing with the logbook. Or, if the matter escalates to something major, you are prepared and ready for what happens. Either way, it doesn't hurt to document everything.

### c.) Seek Guidance from a Friend or Mentor

There are times when sexual harassment may leave you baffled. When you don't know what to do. You might be afraid that no one will believe you, or that they will think it's no big deal. The landscape is often difficult and confusing. You don't want the perpetrator to get away with it, and you are also afraid of the repercussions if you do something about it.

Seeking guidance from a colleague you trust, a friend in the business or one of your mentors can be a huge help in this regard. It is likely they have seen this behavior before. They might have great suggestions on how to deal with it based on their knowledge of the company and the individual. Use their experience to help you navigate your options. You may want to consult several people to get different opinions. The more input you get, the stronger you will feel about your decision on how to respond. The added benefit in getting other peoples' input is that you will let people know that this behavior is not welcome and must not be tolerated.

d.)    Reporting the Incident

There are times when reporting an incident is relatively easy. If, for instance, you are at a conference and the person who made the unwelcome overture is someone who doesn't relate to your business, you can report the matter to the conference organizers, your boss, or even the person's boss.

There are other times when reporting could cause discomfort. What if it involves your direct boss or a well-liked colleague? What if it involves the vice president or president of the company? Ultimately, you have to be comfortable with your actions. Perhaps you can report to a Human Resources person anonymously. Perhaps there is someone else in the company whom you trust, and who can advise you. There are many ways to report the matter. Read your *Employee Handbook* or corporate policy for handling these things. You may be surprised to learn that people will be there to help you. The #Metoo movement has brought a lot of these behaviors to light and has increased the likelihood of consequences for the perpetrators.

The reality is that if we don't report these matters, they will continue. They will happen to other women. Do what feels right and comfortable for your well-being and career.

## e.)   Don't Let the Pattern Continue

I can't stress enough that we have to do everything we can to stop the pattern of sexual harassment in male-dominated businesses. It has to be talked about. We have to take action when it occurs whether we are at the bottom of the totem pole, or whether we are leaders in the field.

When I started working at a large corporation in my younger days, I entered the company as a manager. Both my female and male colleagues would taunt me and say things like, "You must be sleeping with the vice president to get the position you did at age 27." I couldn't believe it. When I confronted the vice president, I said, "The people who work for you think I'm sleeping with you and that's how I got my job, instead of acknowledging that I got this job because I'm good at what I do." His response was, "Did they say whether we were having fun in our affair?"

I was distraught. He then started asking me out on dates and making sexual advances. My next step was to call Human Resources. Unfortunately, Human Resources was intimidated by the vice president and suggested I try yoga to feel better. Yoga? Are you freaking kidding me? Then I threatened the offenders with a lawsuit for harassment, and the harassment stopped. The vice president called me into his office and asked me what the lawsuit was about. I clearly laid out the times I had been sexually harassed or suggested I got the job based on sexual favors. The harassment stopped. I also was moved to another position, which was actually a higher position, where I wouldn't have to deal with those people.

As we move up the career ladder, there are more opportunities to break the pattern of sexual harassment. With power and authority comes accountability. We have to be responsible and accountable for creating a work environment that is inclusive and safe.

One of the female leaders I consulted in writing this book told me an interesting anecdote. She had just become the director of a division in a large corporation. One older male who reported to her was known for sexually harassing his colleagues. For twenty-five years, no one did anything about it. Because his behavior was talked about by the people it affected, everyone knew about it. When he did it again, he was called into the director's office. Although it was a minor incident, she fired him immediately. She told me that she felt she had to fire him to set a precedent. She wanted to send a clear message that this behavior would no longer be tolerated.

Whether you are starting your career or are already at the top, you have a role to play in solving this challenge. If we are truly to become leaders, we need to stand up for everyone—including women who are sexually harassed.

---

In Her Words . . .

My experience being ogled made me double down on my efforts to not stand out from the men. It's taken me nearly 20 years to get over this, and it's still something that I work on.

My advice to young women is to be yourself. If you're feminine, be feminine. If you're not, don't be. If you're bossy, be bossy. If you're quiet, that's fine too. People will judge you no matter what – so you might as well be yourself. The more you can be yourself, the more confident you'll be, and the more confident you are, the more successful you'll be. There isn't a single path to success. You have to find the path for you.

*Gale Hauck, Deputy Site Director Sector: Nuclear Power*

---

In the next chapter, we'll learn more about how to use your natural skills as a woman to get ahead and succeed in your career.

# CHAPTER 10

## How Women Are Natural
## Leaders in the Workplace

In her book *Why the Best Man for the Job is a Woman: The Unique Female Qualities of Leadership,* Esther Wachs says, "a new breed of leader is emerging, and that breed is female."[9] The world of business is changing, and this is particularly good news for women, especially in male-dominated fields.

Isn't it interesting that when women enter a workplace in droves, things seem to change? People tend to be more respectful of others. Collaboration occurs more frequently. Business relationships get formed more easily.

Although we are so often told that women don't have what it takes in male-dominated businesses, we are actually very well equipped to be business leaders. Our natural abilities make us great leaders for many reasons. We have a more collaborative leadership style; we tend to communicate well; we are good at handling crises; we see the bigger picture, and we are great at building relationships and networking. All of this enables us to get better business results.

### We Tend to Use a Collaborative Approach

Women are natural collaborators. We buy into the notion that the entire team needs to work well together to realize the desired positive business results. Typically, when faced with a challenge, we combine various resources with different areas of expertise. And so we tackle the problem together and create a solution. In contrast, men in male-dominated sectors tend to be more self-centered when working toward success. They will try to fix the problem by themselves and not reach out for help. Since competition is the norm in these businesses, people tend to hoard their ideas to be perceived as the lone wolf who alone comes up with the solution and gets the glory.

When two or more people come together in business to share ideas and skills, magic tends to happen. Productivity soars since everyone is sharing their experience and know-how, and creating a competent talent pool based on different skills. Employees tend to be happier because relationships are promoted and encouraged. Team work enables employees to work quickly, which leads to efficiency and time saving. Creativity increases. Employees feel more valued due to the higher level of collaboration. And ultimately, collaboration results in faster and better problem solving.

From what my colleagues and I have observed, women tend to more consistently use collaboration. *A Harvard Business Review* article ("In Collaborative Work Cultures, Women Carry More of the Weight" July 24, 2018)[10] explains why. According to their research, women are more likely to care for the community of individuals they work with. If there is ambiguity, we tend to step in and try to smooth things over. Our focus tends to be on the collective good, rather than focusing only on our role and our immediate work. The environment fostered is more cooperative and less authoritarian.

Increasingly, businesses are using more collaborative platforms to fulfil their goals. The ability to work well in a team is highly valued in a significant number of workplaces, particularly in high-stress environments. As natural relationship builders and cooperators, we are able to leverage our collaborative nature to benefit the company as a whole and to become transformational leaders.

## We Are Great Communicators

Haven't you heard this before? Women are great communicators. Why? Well, maybe being the center of family life for thousands of years has taught us that we have to communicate well to make sure that everyone around us is moving in the same direction to achieve a common goal—even if it's staying alive when lions are chasing us.

We tend to communicate often with everyone. In my experience, we tend to express ourselves verbally more than men. We are also great at listening and hearing other people's opinions and insights. Our regular discussions with the people around us is an important factor in our success. It allows for more exchange of learning and ideas. It helps us spread the word about what it will take to achieve success in business. Our excellent communication skills allow us to outline our visions to our colleagues and motivate others to join us in solving problems. And when people get motivated to solve problems, the chances of achieving success skyrocket.

When it comes to getting others to act, women can be great motivators based on our communication skills. We are often able to clearly articulate what needs to get done and the reasons "why" things need to be done. It's the "why" that gets people moving. Our passion in communicating with others can be infectious. It can lead others to share our passion and get the job done with enthusiasm.

## We Tend to Handle Crises Well

As women and as moms, we are often faced with a variety of crises, from toddler meltdowns to negotiating terms of agreements to get teenagers to empty the dishwasher. We are hit with rough situations from all sides, including work, family, careers and household issues. Sometimes, we are forced to go from one crisis to another in the same day and in different areas of our lives. How do we do it?

I can tell you from experience in male-dominated fields that women tend to keep their anger in check more often than men. This is not to say we don't get angry. We do. However, we tend to funnel our anger (for the most part) in a way to resolve the situation, instead of lashing out. Take a toddler meltdown for instance. What would a woman do? She would likely (after rolling her eyes) get down on her knees and speak compassionately with the toddler, understand their needs and come up with a solution to make the toddler feel better. Or, if she does get angry, she still has to work with the toddler in some way to bring resolution. Women have never had the luxury of failure.

It's no surprise then that when it comes to handling a crisis at work, we take it all in stride. Women tend to listen to the people around them when they are in a difficult situation. We reach out to people to get advice. We try to help everyone work together to find the answer to the problem. Even if we are upset, we tend (for the most part) to show up and help negotiate a successful result that pleases the most people. Our desire to overcome difficult situations fuels us. It makes us better at finding our way to a solution.

## We Are *Amazing* Multi-Taskers[11]

How many things do you juggle in one day? I'm going to assume it is a lot, since you're reading this book. You are probably one of those wonderful go-getter people with a full schedule of meetings and activities.

As women, we have a number of facets of our lives that we must handle. We juggle our careers with a host of other responsibilities. Along with our work, we:

- Cook dinners.
- Raise our kids.
- Negotiate disagreements between family members. (*"Yes, you have to share that package of cookies with your sister, or else I'm taking them away from you."*)
- Do things to make our partners happy and keep the fire alive in our relationship.
- Do the laundry (which never ends).
- Clean the house (which never ends).
- Walk the dogs. Every. Damn. Day.

- Ensure everyone's doctors' appointments are kept.
- Enroll the kids in the activities they want, no matter how crazy. (*"So, you want to take underwater basket weaving lessons?"*)
- Drive the kids to their respective activities.
- Help our kids with homework.
- Attend parent-teacher conferences.
- Organize birthday parties and family holidays.
- Plan vacations.
- Keep up with our friendships.
- Find time for ourselves to read, paint or do whatever makes us happy.

Whew! I'm exhausted just looking at that list. Yet, somehow, we tend to take it all in stride. For the most part, at least. Of course, some days are better than others. Sometimes we wish we could have a little bit more help. In this day and age, our husbands or life partners are taking up more of the burden of running the family. All in all, though, we make it through, and our world is better off for it.

The ability to multi-task helps us incredibly in business. We are able to take on many different things and somehow manage them all. For instance, we can handle multiple projects and deliverables at the same time. Our focus tends to be holistic, rather than laser pointed on a single object. Because of this, we are able to pivot from one area of our life to another with relative ease.

Don't get me wrong. Some tasks require laser focus. This is where men thrive and where we can learn from them. Men tend to be amazing at focusing on one area and doing it really well. But business can be competitive and hectic, particularly in male-dominated fields.

When it comes to succeeding in business, women's ability to manage a variety of things allows us to be efficient. After all, time is money. If we can save time by doing many things at once, we are ultimately increasing the productivity and competitiveness of the business.

**In Her Words . . .**

Your advantages over your male colleagues: You know how to multi-task.

You know how to empathize and relate with both men and women. Men tend to only be able to see things from their own perspectives. I can count on one hand the number of men I've met who can deeply empathize. They are normally exceptional HR managers and executive coaches.

In order to be successful in life, school and business, you've had to try harder than most men. You are therefore resilient. If you're knocked down, you pick yourself up and carry on. You won't take a hit, punch or a "no" without fighting. Those scars are the building blocks that will ultimately lead to your success.

*Submitted by: Carolyn Preston, CEO. Sector: Oil & Gas*

**We See the Big Picture**

There is a tendency for women to see the forest *and* the trees. We see the big picture as opposed to being bogged down in the details.

This can be seen especially in the world of engineering. Male engineers I have worked with often go down a rabbit hole when they have a new idea or innovation. As a leader of a company, it is my job to ensure that these shiny new trinkets that the engineers get excited about have a viable business market to sell into. I need to ensure that their exciting engineering projects will actually make money and be profitable. If no profit is projected for a great idea, it doesn't go ahead.

(On a side note, there is a hilarious example of engineers designing and developing a new piece of equipment that would make maintenance of a power plant much more time and cost effective. Not one of the design engineers asked themselves whether the equipment would fit through the door to the plant. It didn't. Hence, the need for seeing the big picture.)

I was once consulting for an engineering company with declining revenues. They needed a real boost to their bottom line. They brought me into a large boardroom with their senior leadership and showed me a list of areas where they were focusing their efforts. Then, they asked me which of those areas of business they should pursue. I spent some time analyzing the amount of time they spent on each of the areas, how profitable each area of business was, and what the market forecast was for each of those areas.

I returned to the boardroom and delivered the shocking news. I told them to scrap everything they had been focusing on. Immediately. I showed them my analysis which demonstrated that the most senior and best paid engineers were working on *volunteering* their time on really cool yet completely unprofitable engineering challenges. The return on investment for their time would likely not come for another ten years or longer, if at all. And they had only six months of payroll left! They were not seeing the forest for the trees.

Although I knew the customer would not like it, I told them to cease and desist all work and activity in the shiny, new, cool area. They needed, instead, to focus on the parts of their business that were actually making money. Even though these areas of business were less "sexy," they were more lucrative and had a much better forecast for growth. If they were going to turn the company around, they had to make this change. I recently reconnected with my customer and was pleased to learn that they took my advice. They are now cash-flow positive and very successful.

Women make great leaders because we tend to see the big picture, challenge traditional assumptions and inspire people to take action. We know how to take big ideas and communicate them to move things along in order to achieve a successful outcome.

**We Focus on Building Long-Term Relationships**

Business is all about relationships. Relationships with our customers. Relationships with our employees. Relationships with our suppliers, industry associations and boards. In order to be a successful leader, a person has to build, manage and maintain these relationships while moving the company toward a successful goal.

When I first joined the company I'm leading now, one of the first questions I asked was, "What's your marketing strategy?"

The answer I got wasn't satisfactory. They said: "We don't do any marketing. People just come to us because they know us and we do good work."

I often hear that from male-dominated businesses. They say things like, "*We did one week of marketing in 1982 and that has sustained us until now.*" When I ask what their future looks like, they can't answer. The world has changed significantly, especially in recent years. The old idea of building a better mouse-trap to get business no longer holds true. These days, you need to constantly build trust with customers and develop lasting relationships with influencers to have ongoing and sustainable business profitability.

The company I now run never visited their customers before I got there. They had little to no outlook into what customers planned to spend with us over the upcoming months or years. All communication was done over the phone or email, and only on an as-needed basis. We belonged to very few industry associations, and did not have insight into industry and market trends.

One of the first changes I made was to personally visit our top five customers. I genuinely wanted to get to know them and help them. These people were the ones who were helping feed my family and stay afloat. I wanted to build a relationship with them that went beyond the traditional phone call when they needed us. So, I booked the executive team tickets to visit all our top customers. This was a pricey business development tour that took us across the U.S., Europe and Canada.

The payback was enormous. Within a year of engaging with customers on a more personal basis, we increased our top line revenues by 50% and our profitability went up by 5%. All this was from using an innate ability to connect with people and show them we care.

By focusing on relationships, women have an ability to create long-term and ongoing business success. We are doing more than chasing each lead as it comes in. Rather, we are programmed to pre-emptively build strategic partnerships with key customers. The partnerships help us achieve our goals while we help customers achieve theirs. We seek a win-win for both parties, which is critical for a company's long-term viability.

## We Are Whizzes at Networking

One of my clients during my consulting years was completely new to the world of networking and business development. They sorely needed new business to survive. This automotive company had hired me to help them diversify into new business sectors. There was a conference on mass transit--an adjacent sector--and I decided to take the all-male executive team to the conference to pursue new business.

The opening night of the conference featured a networking reception, as most conferences do. As soon as they arrived, they ordered their beers and saw a beautiful leather sofa that no one was sitting on. They all went and sat on the sofa and started talking among themselves. When I saw what was going on, I pushed my way through to them, looked at them sternly and said, "*What part of prostitution did you not understand?*" Although my words were harsh, they got the message. They got up and started to walk around the room and talking to people. The whole point of a networking event is to meet new people who can help you, not sit around talking among yourselves.

The vast majority of women are naturals at being social. Maybe it's because we have to deal with parent-teacher conferences. Maybe it's because we earned money by babysitting in our teens. Whatever the reason, we tend to be great at socializing and networking.

To me, there is no better or more important skill than networking. Networking allows you to go beyond the realm of your immediate colleagues and expand your horizon to new people and new ideas. People who are good at networking in business have more job opportunities, are better recognized in their fields, and tend to move up the career ladder faster than those who aren't great at it. Why? People who are great at networking are also great at being seen. If you are seen around industry, people will know you. When people know you, they will support you and help you.

In our next chapter, we'll go through the lessons learned from this book and give final tips and tricks to fast-track your career.

# CHAPTER 11

## Getting from A to B Elegantly and Based on Merit (You've Got This!)

You made it! Congratulations! Few people finish reading a book that can help them succeed in life, so I want to thank you and tell you I'm proud of you for staying with it.

I hope you have learned from this book and will remember: *Believe in Yourself.* You've decided to be in a high stress environment and a male-dominated field for a reason. You are a go-getter. You don't go with the flow, but you stand above the crowd and you are a trailblazer. Give yourself the credit you deserve.

---

In Her Words . . .

In every workplace, there are those that have biases who could prevent you from directing your career the way you want. The trick is to not let them derail you from doing what you know is right for you.

The physical barriers, such as a lack of bathrooms or change rooms for women, may have changed thanks to laws that ensure such equitable access. However, attitudinal barriers can remain. The key is not to let others' opinions affect your work.

---

> At the end of the day, you are the only one in charge of the direction you take. Others' opinions are simply obstacles to be navigated.
>
> For me, career paths are what you want them to be. My path was not a straight line, there were twists and turns along the way. There were even some pretty big stop signs.
>
> What one must do is learn from each twist, turn or stop. Own the outcome, remake yourself, get better and go further.
>
> *Laurie Swami, President and CEO at Nuclear Waste Management Organization*

It's a difficult world out there in business. Women in male-dominated businesses have it particularly rough. Yet, despite the odds women are thriving and succeeding in these industries and you can too. By using the strategies and tactics in this book, you too can fast track your career and achieve your goals.

Where do you start? You start at the beginning—you. You are the foundation of your own success. Do my exercises to reprogram your beliefs. Boost your confidence, even if you don't feel it. Shore up everything in you to believe that success is yours for the taking and moreover, that you deserve it and are worthy.

Set goals for yourself. Imagine a bright future where you are the one in charge.

Know your stuff. Yes, you'll have to work harder than your male counterparts. You wouldn't be in this field if you didn't think that was the case. So, do your homework. Learn all the ins and outs of the business, including the technical stuff. Show colleagues that you can handle difficult situations by having the necessary information to make good business decisions.

When addressing a challenge, make sure you have the facts and evidence in hand before approaching your colleagues. If you only approach people with problems, you'll be seen as part of the problem. If you approach them with a solution that's backed up by facts and evidence, you will be seen as part of the solution.

Show up every day knowing you are a successful leader. You'll be amazed at how people treat you when you show confidence and take credit for your accomplishments. Use your natural talents to handle the work coming your way. Do it with grace and elegance. Finally, show people that they are dealing with a smart, hard-working and wonderful person who will succeed and bring them along for the ride.

That's what leadership--in any business--is all about.

The more you use the techniques in this book and the more you step up, the greater your chances of getting ahead based on your worth and accomplishments. You'll be recognized as a person who brings people together to face challenges head-on and succeed with elegance.

Things will inevitably get in your way. People will be rude. Challenges and roadblocks will appear. When this happens, hold your head high and remember to be the queen that you are. Keep your stuff together and address the situation calmly and logically.

Remember, you got this girl!

Now go out there and succeed!

# ACKNOWLEDGEMENTS

This book could not have happened without the love and support of several people. First, I wish to thank my amazing children, Amelia and Troy, who continuously gave me the encouragement I needed and who constantly reminded me of the importance of this work. You are my reason for getting up in the morning. Thank you also to my partner in crime and love of my life, Brent, for your unbreakable love, encouragement and understanding. Thank you to my parents Janet and Joseph, my brother Shant, and my sister in spirit Meline, for all of their support.

I wish to thank my beta readers for giving me early encouragement and feedback on the book, including Carolyn Preston, Gale Hauck, Shaian Mollaret and Pierre and Linda Yeremian. You helped me find my own voice.

Thank you to all the contributors to the book including: Brenda Andress, Gale Hauck, Carolyn Preston, Jenna Shaw, Erin Wehlage, Laurie Swami, Rachna Clavero, Michele Cheung-Newson, Jacqui D'Eon, Marion Fraser, Catherine Prat, Yolanda Troxell, Janet Wardle, Eva Martinez and Randi Thomson. I am a better person for having known you all. The book would not have been the same without you.

Thank you to my editor Quata Diann Merit, who's tireless work made my words sing.

Thank you to my cheerleading squad who encouraged me to succeed throughout the years, even when I didn't think it was possible. This includes (but is not limited to): Hasmig Adjelian, Klaus Büttner, Glen

Hodgson, Art Wharton, Chad Boyer, Piyush Sabharwall, Brett Rampal, John Muir, Brigitte Svarich Muir, Sandra Sloan, Frank Helin, Deano Helin, Val Wilson, Leigh Krauss, Paul Eric Marko, Lindsay McMurray and all the members of TEC620, Terry Ann Cofer-Adamo, Ed Wolbert, Jeanetta Vena, John Bifolchi and Carmen Young, Lavinia Litras, Kareen Martin, Jody Squires (for his hilarious analysis of alpha and beta males using salt and pepper shakers), Sam Wong for his amazing photography, Cynthia Barlow, Cassandra Drudi, Jerry Hopwood, Parry Walborn, and Chantal Kahale.

Thank you to Joshua Sprague. Your 30 day book writing challenge is what got me going. Thank you for reading early drafts of my work and encouraging me to keep writing no matter what.

Last but not least, thank you to those people who tried to stand in the way of me succeeding in my career. Without you, this book would not be possible.

# DEDICATION

This book is dedicated to the fourteen women (twelve engineering students, one nursing student, and one employee of the university) who were shot and killed at the École Polytechnique in Montreal.

On December 6, 1989, a shooter (I refuse to include his name) separated nine women from the approximately fifty men in the room and ordered the men to leave. He asked the remaining women whether they knew why they were there. When one student replied, *"No,"* He answered, *"I am fighting feminism."* One of the students, Nathalie Provost, said, *"Look, we are just women studying engineering, not necessarily feminists ready to march on the streets to shout we are against men, just students intent on leading a normal life."* he responded, *"You're women. You're going to be engineers. You're all a bunch of feminists. I hate feminists."*

He opened fire on the students, then continued his rampage throughout the building targeting his shootings on mostly women.

The victims were:

- Geneviève Bergeron (born 1968), civil engineering student
- Hélène Colgan (born 1966), mechanical engineering student
- Nathalie Croteau (born 1966), mechanical engineering student
- Barbara Daigneault (born 1967), mechanical engineering student
- Anne-Marie Edward (born 1968), chemical engineering student
- Maud Haviernick (born 1960), materials engineering student
- Maryse Laganière (born 1964), budget clerk in the École Polytechnique's finance department

- Maryse Leclair (born 1966), materials engineering student
- Anne-Marie Lemay (born 1967), mechanical engineering student
- Sonia Pelletier (born 1961), mechanical engineering student
- Michèle Richard (born 1968), materials engineering student
- Annie St-Arneault (born 1966), mechanical engineering student
- Annie Turcotte (born 1969), materials engineering student
- Barbara Klucznik-Widajewicz (born 1958), nursing student

May we never forget them.

May we succeed in male-dominated fields so that their sacrifice will not have been in vain.

May we build a future so that women around the world will never again be frightened to enter and thrive in technical fields of work.

Rosemary Yeremian, December 6, 2020

# ENDNOTES

1 Covid refers to the pandemic of Covid-19, the 2020 global pandemic that also resulted in a significant economic downturn.

2 Sandberg, Sheryl. *Lean In : Women, Work, and the Will to Lead*. New York, New York: Random House Audio, 2013

3 Barbara Stocking, "Workplace Culture Alienates Women," *Financial Times*, August 24, 2016

4 Susan Chira, "The Universal Phenomenon of Men Interrupting Women," *New York Times*, June 14, 2017.

5 Heilman, Madeline E., Haynes, Michelle C., "No Credit Where Credit Is Due: Attributional Rationalization of Women's Success in Male-Female Teams.", *Journal of Applied Psychology*, Vol 90(5), Sep 2005, 905-916

6 "Advancing the Future of Women in Business | The 2020 KPMG Women's Leadership Summit Report", 2020 KPMG International Cooperative, https://womensleadership.kpmg.us/summit.html

7 New America, *"Breaking Into the Blue-Collar Boys' Club: Male-Dominated, Low- and Middle-Wage Sectors,"* https://www.newamerica.org/better-life-lab/reports/sexual-harassment-severe-and-pervasive-problem/breaking-into-the-blue-collar-boys-club-male-dominated-low-and-middle-wage-sectors/, retrieved on Dec. 5, 2020.

8 "Women in the Workplace 2018", McKinsey & Company, Lean In.org, https://womenintheworkplace.com/2018#!

9 Wachs, Esther, *Why the Best Man for the Job Is a Woman: The Unique Female Qualities of Leadership*, HarperCollins, 2000.

10 Cullinan, Renee, "In Collaborative Work Cultures, Women Carry More of the Weight", *Harvard Business Review*, July 24, 2018

11 There are conflicting studies about gender differences in multi-tasking. A widely held view is that women tend to be better at it. This is supported by several research studies, including: Stoet, G., O'Connor, D.B., Conner, M. et al. *"Are women better than men at multi-tasking?"*. BMC Psychol 1, 18 (2013). https://doi.org/10.1186/2050-7283-1-18. Based on my personal experience working in male-dominated businesses, I have noticed a tendency for women to better handle multiple tasks at a time in high-stress environments, when compared with men.

# SOURCES

"Advancing the Future of Women in Business | The 2020 KPMG Women's Leadership Summit Report", 2020 KPMG International Cooperative, https://womensleadership.kpmg.us/summit.html

Agarwal, Dr. Pragya, "*Is The Workplace Culture Stalling Women's Progress*", www.forbes.com, Jun 28, 2019.

"Breaking Into the Blue-Collar Boys' Club: Male-Dominated, Low- and Middle-Wage Sectors," New America, https://www.newamerica.org/better-life-lab/reports/sexual-harassment-severe-and-pervasive-problem/breaking-into-the-blue-collar-boys-club-male-dominated-low-and-middle-wage-sectors/, retrieved on Dec. 5, 2020.

Bohnet, Iris, "*What Works: Gender Equality by Design*", Belknap Press, March 8, 2016. https://www.catalyst.org/research/women-in-male-dominated-industries-and-occupations/#:~:text=In%20the%20United%20States%2C%20only,male%2Ddominated%20occupations%20in%202018.&text=Women's%20job%20growth%20is%20driven,consisting%20of%20two%2Dthirds%20men.

Catalyst, *Quick Take: Women in Management* (August 11, 2020). Retried from: https://www.catalyst.org/research/women-in-management/

Chira, Susan "The Universal Phenomenon of Men Interrupting Women," New York Times, June 14, 2017.

Cullinan, Renee, "In Collaborative Work Cultures, Women Carry More of the Weight", *Harvard Business Review*, July 24, 2018

Daskal, Lolly, "*10 Powerful Ways Woman Can Succeed in a Male-Dominated World*", www.inc.com, Jan. 22, 2018.

Dayton, Denise, "*Careers That Are Male Dominated*", www.houstonchronicle.com, Updated August 21, 2020

Dingfelder, S. "*Women who succeed in male-dominated careers are often seen negatively, suggests study*", American Psychological Association, July/August 2004, Vol 35, No. 7.

Gender Equality Funds website: https://genderequalityfunds.org/gender-equality-workplace?gclid=CjwKCAjw5p_8BRBUEiwAPpJO6zXsaz7Mg VDkgsEup_duGwHZuoy6hOO0686eJRzhEl6uuVR9pQc0gjhoC1lMQ AvD_BwE retrieved on Dec. 6, 2020.

Heilman, Madeline E.,Haynes, Michelle C., "No Credit Where Credit Is Due: Attributional Rationalization of Women's Success in Male-Female Teams.", *Journal of Applied Psychology*, Vol 90(5), Sep 2005, 905-916

Ho, Jackleyn, "*Women Are Moving Into Historically Male Jobs, and Especially Into These 5 Roles*", www.inc.com, March 8, 2018.

"*Male-dominated workplace culture alienates talented women*", Forbes.com

Sandberg, Sheryl. *Lean In : Women, Work, and the Will to Lead. New York*, New York: Random House Audio, 2013

Stocking, Barbara "Workplace Culture Alienates Women," *Financial Times*, August 24, 2016

Stoet, G., O'Connor, D.B., Conner, M. et al. "*Are women better than men at multi-tasking?*". BMC Psychol 1, 18 (2013). https://doi.org/10.1186/2050-7283-1-18.

von Stiegel, Herta, *"Female Leadership In a Male-Dominated World"*, www. forbes.com, Dec 30, 2019.

Wachs, Esther, *Why the Best Man for the Job Is a Woman: The Unique Female Qualities of Leadership*, HarperCollins, 2000.

"Women in the Workplace 2018", McKinsey & Company, Lean In.org, https://womenintheworkplace.com/2018#!